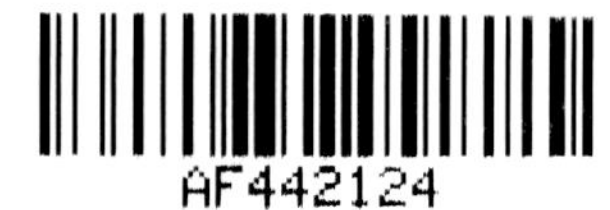

THIS COLORING BOOK
BELONGS TO :

____

- -

____

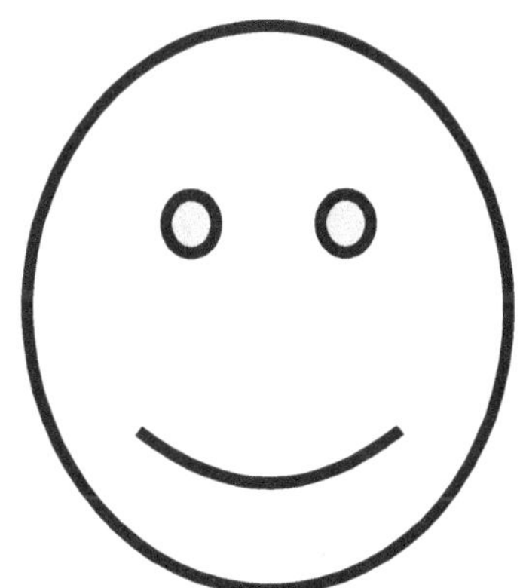

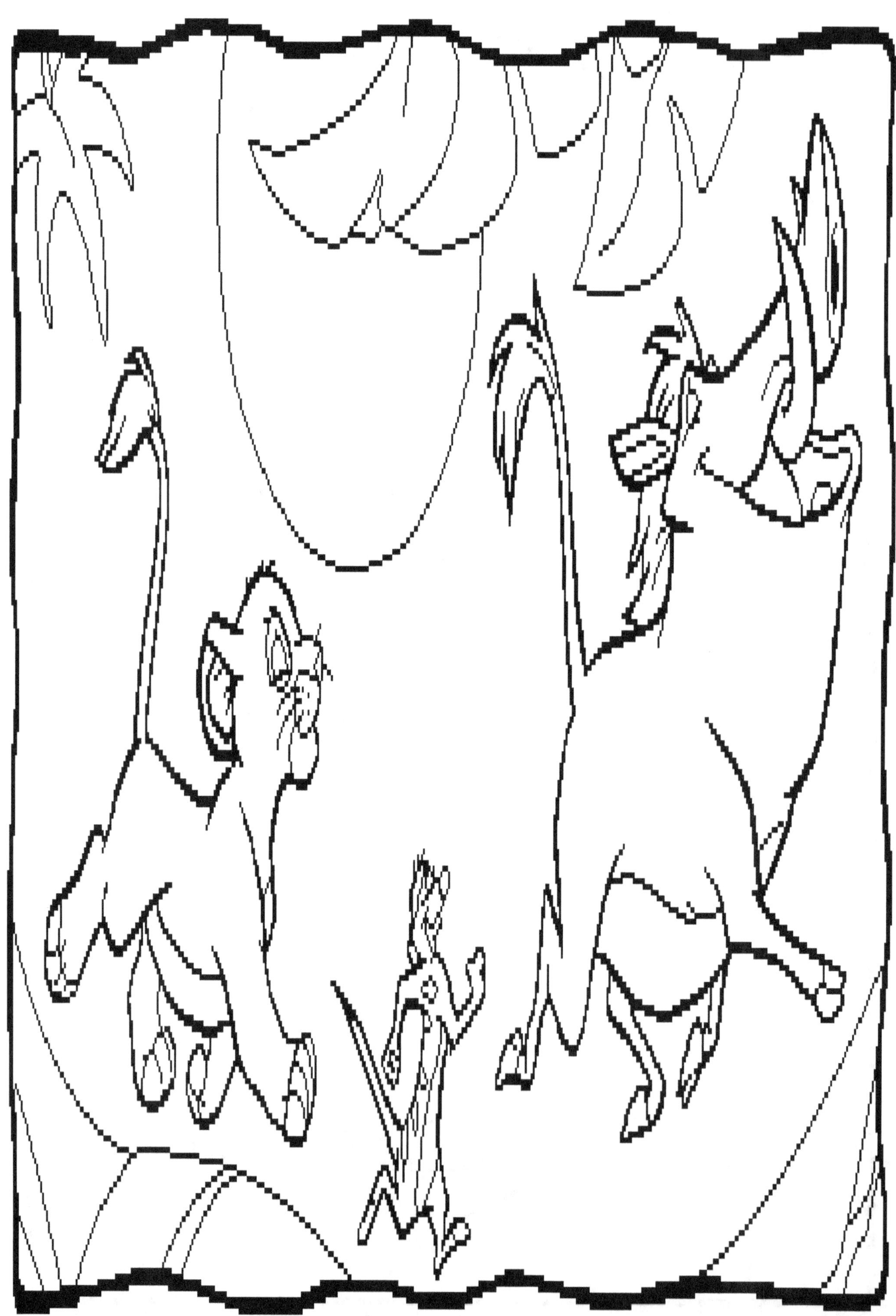

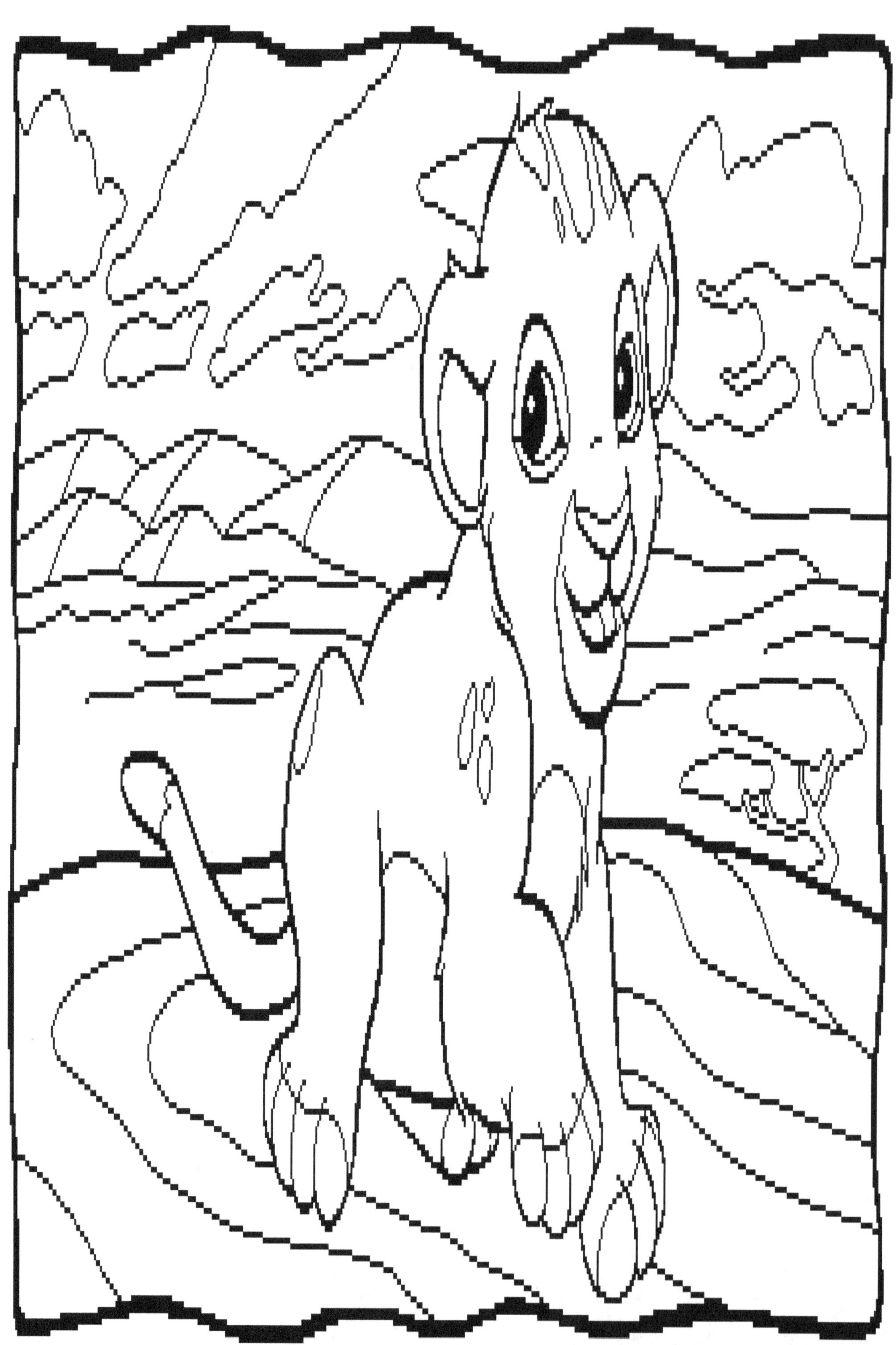

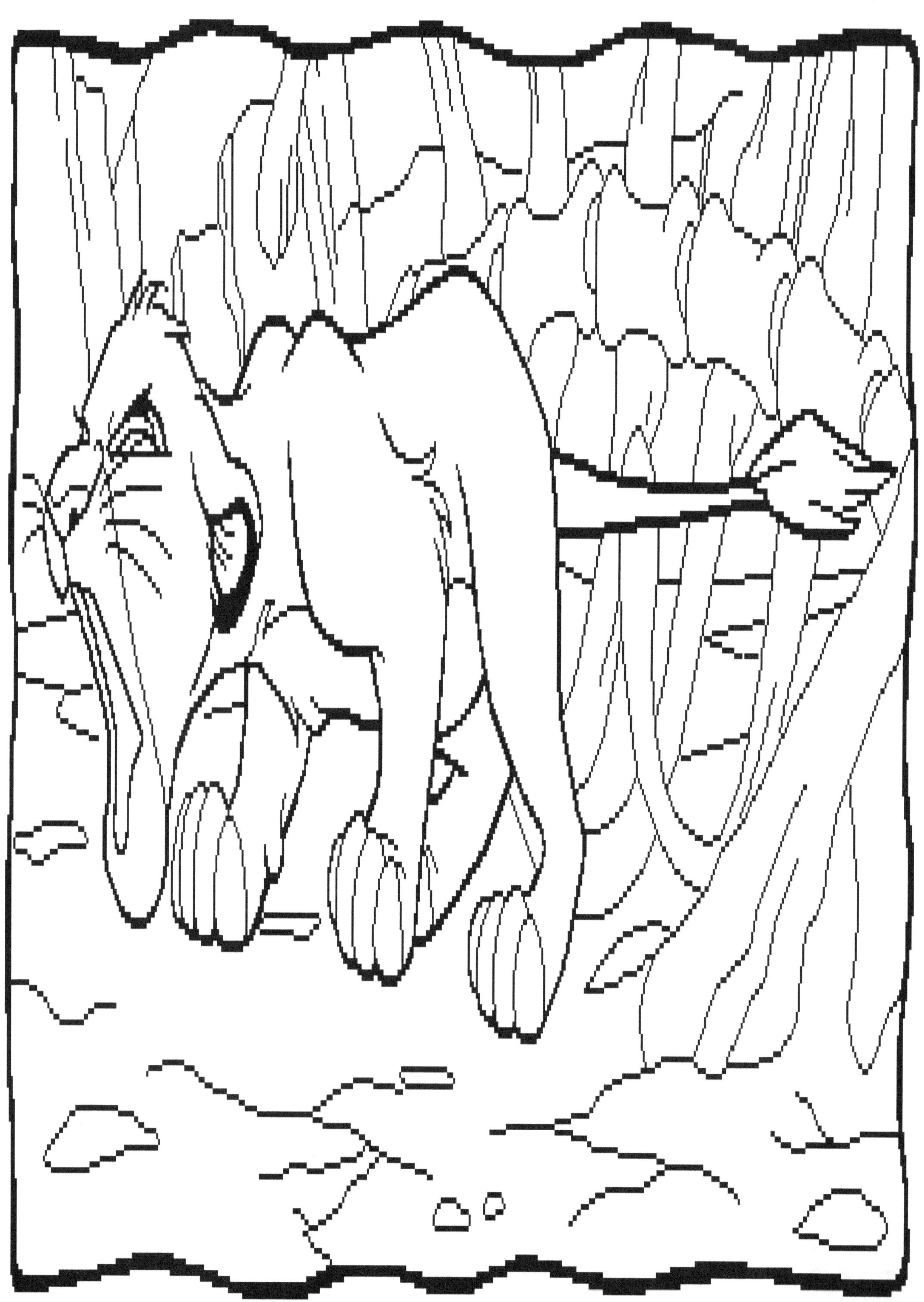

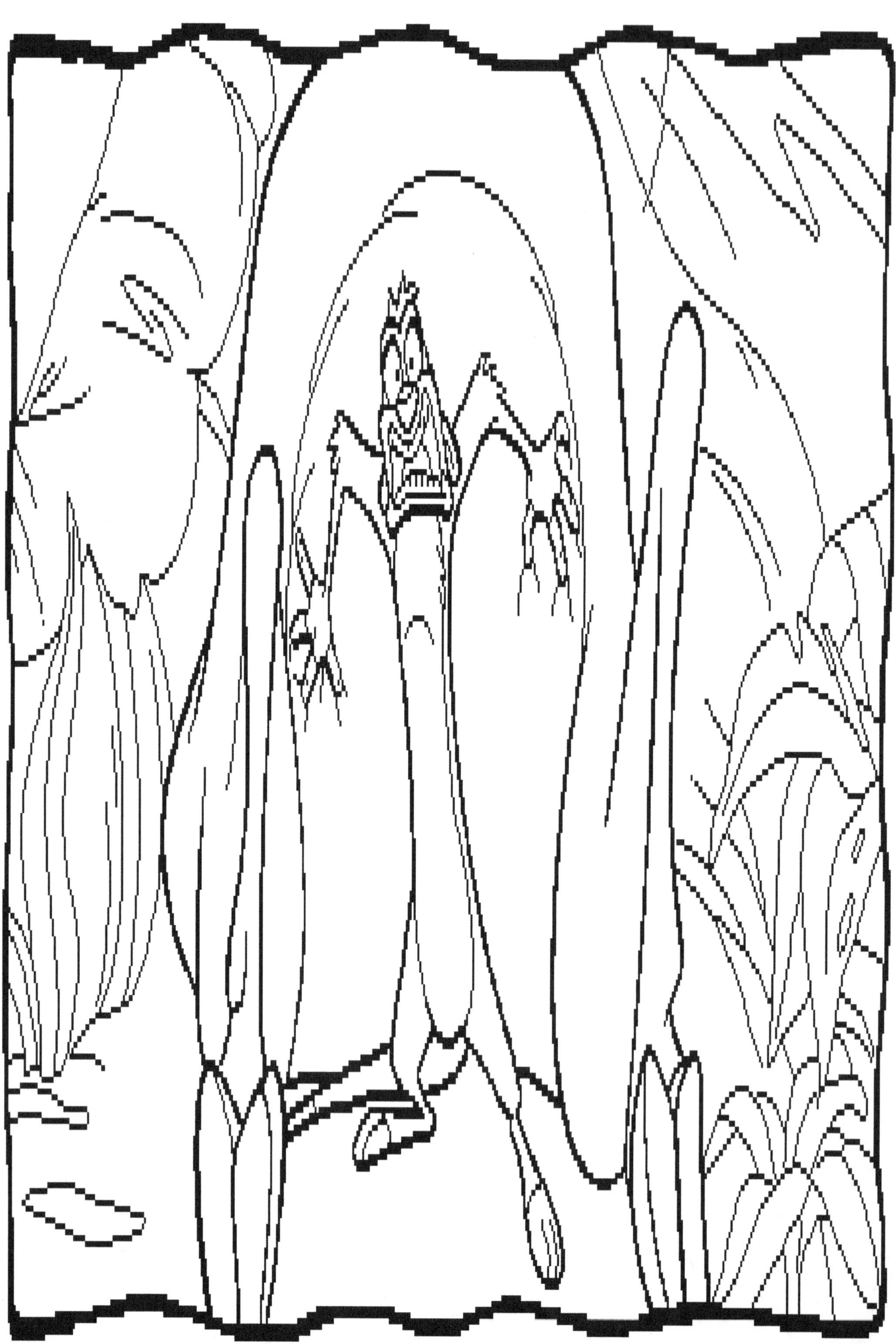

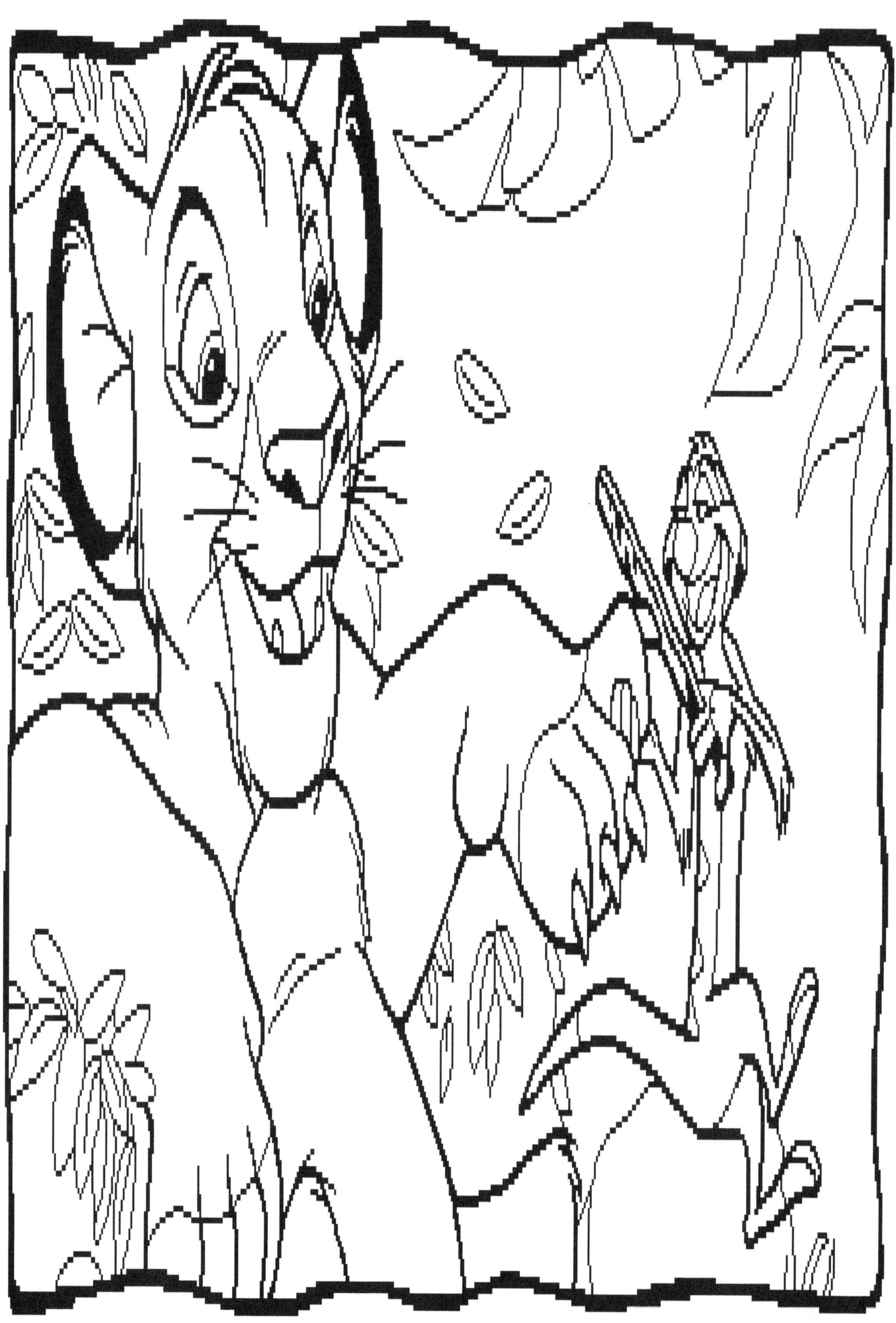

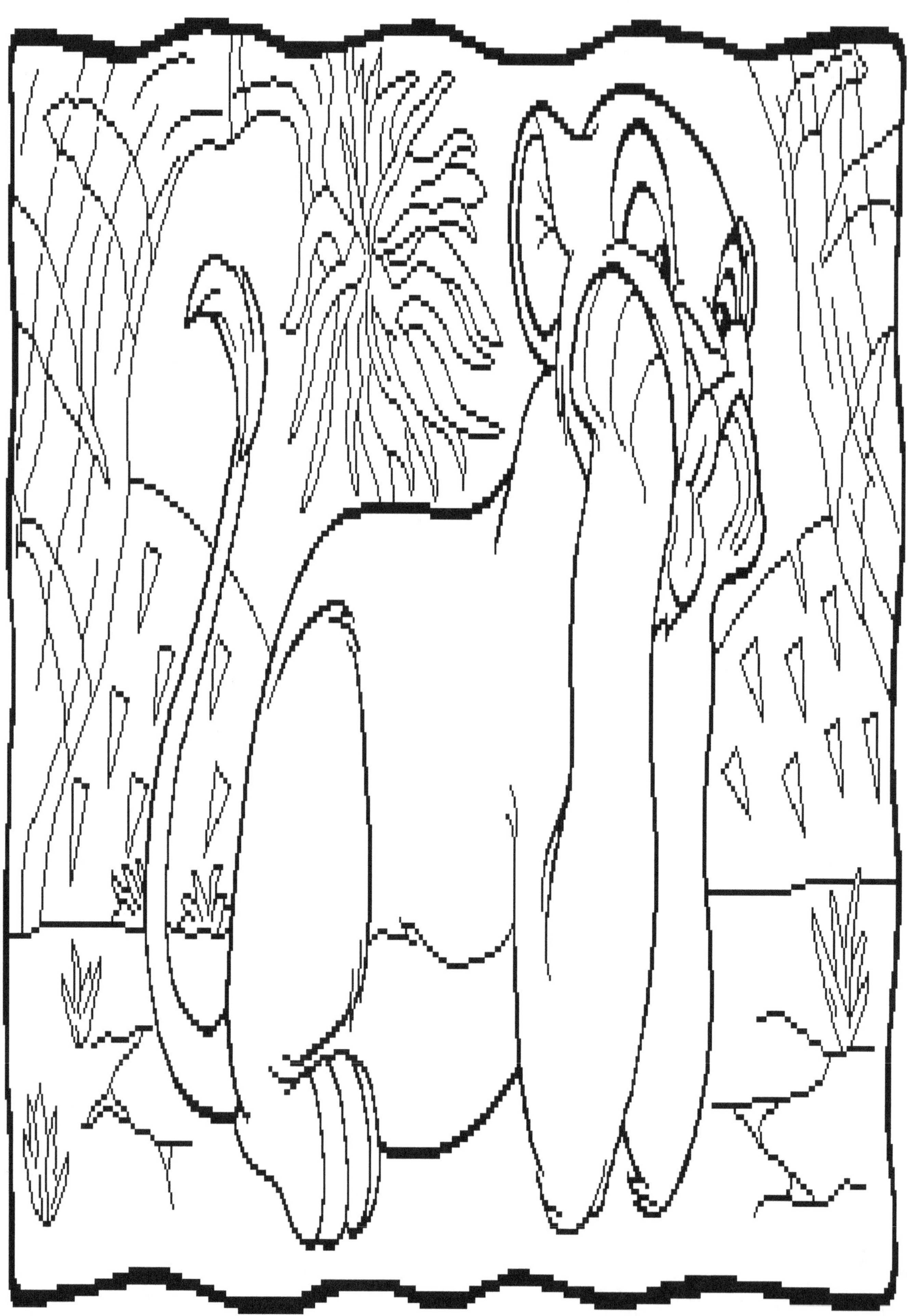

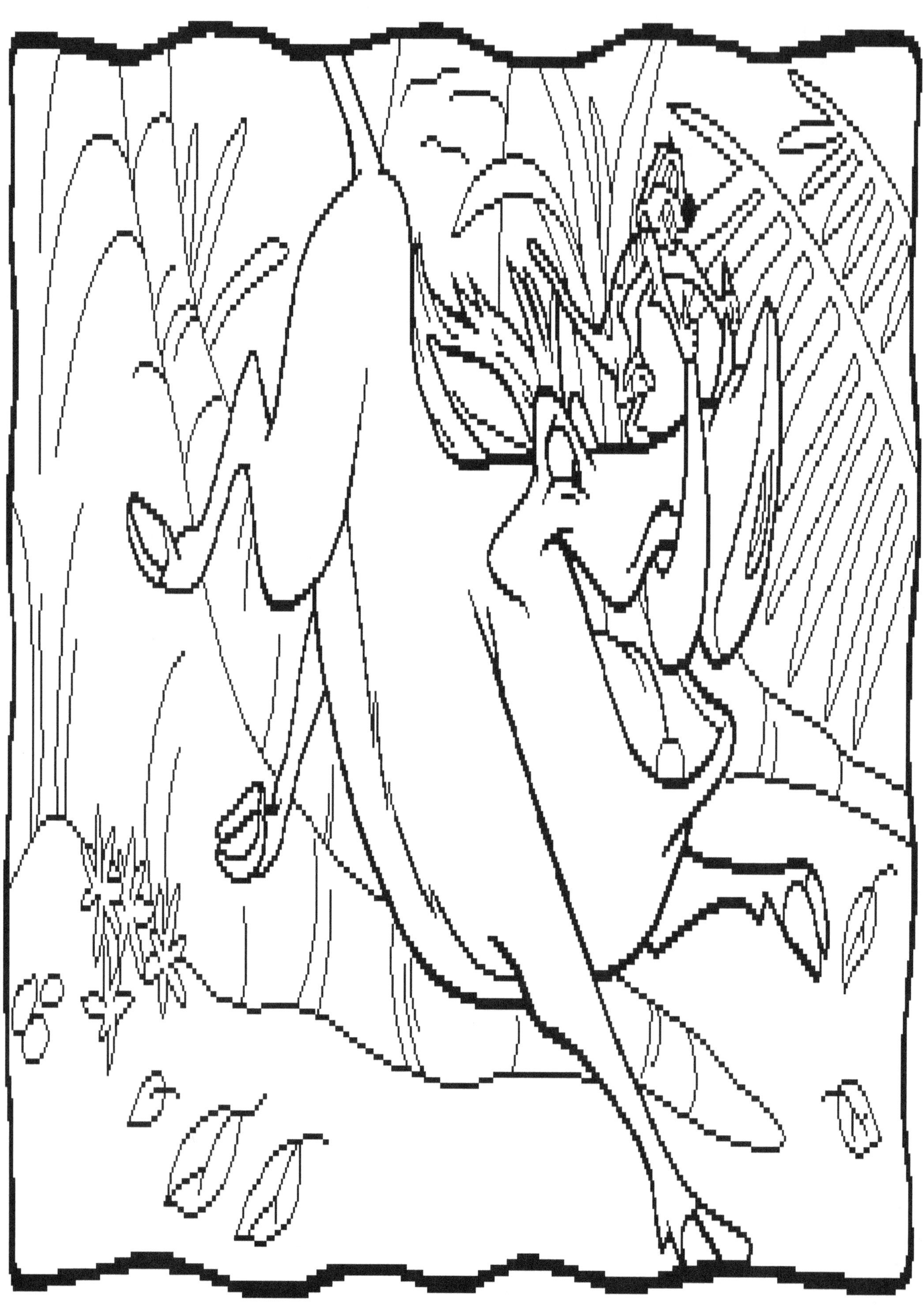

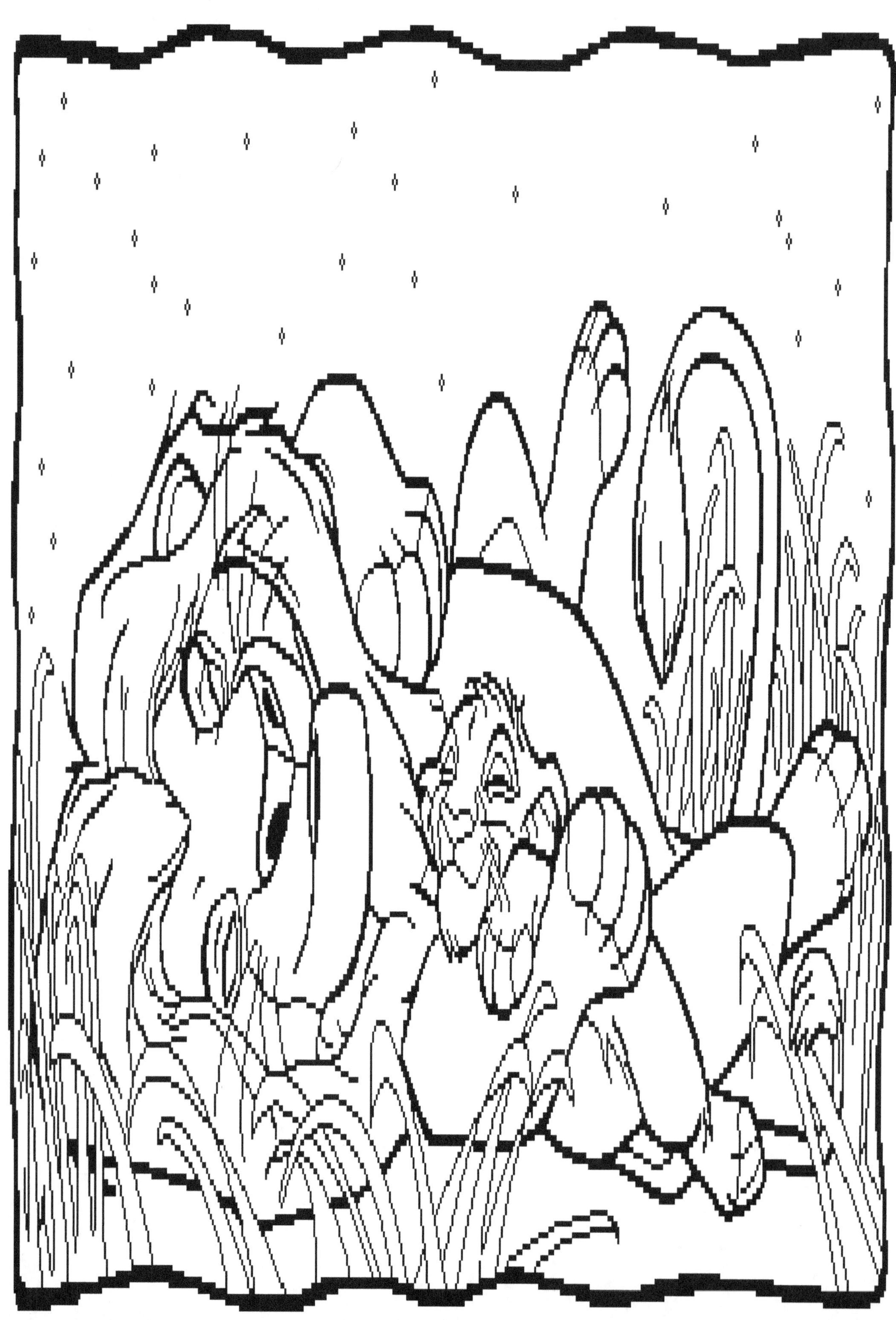

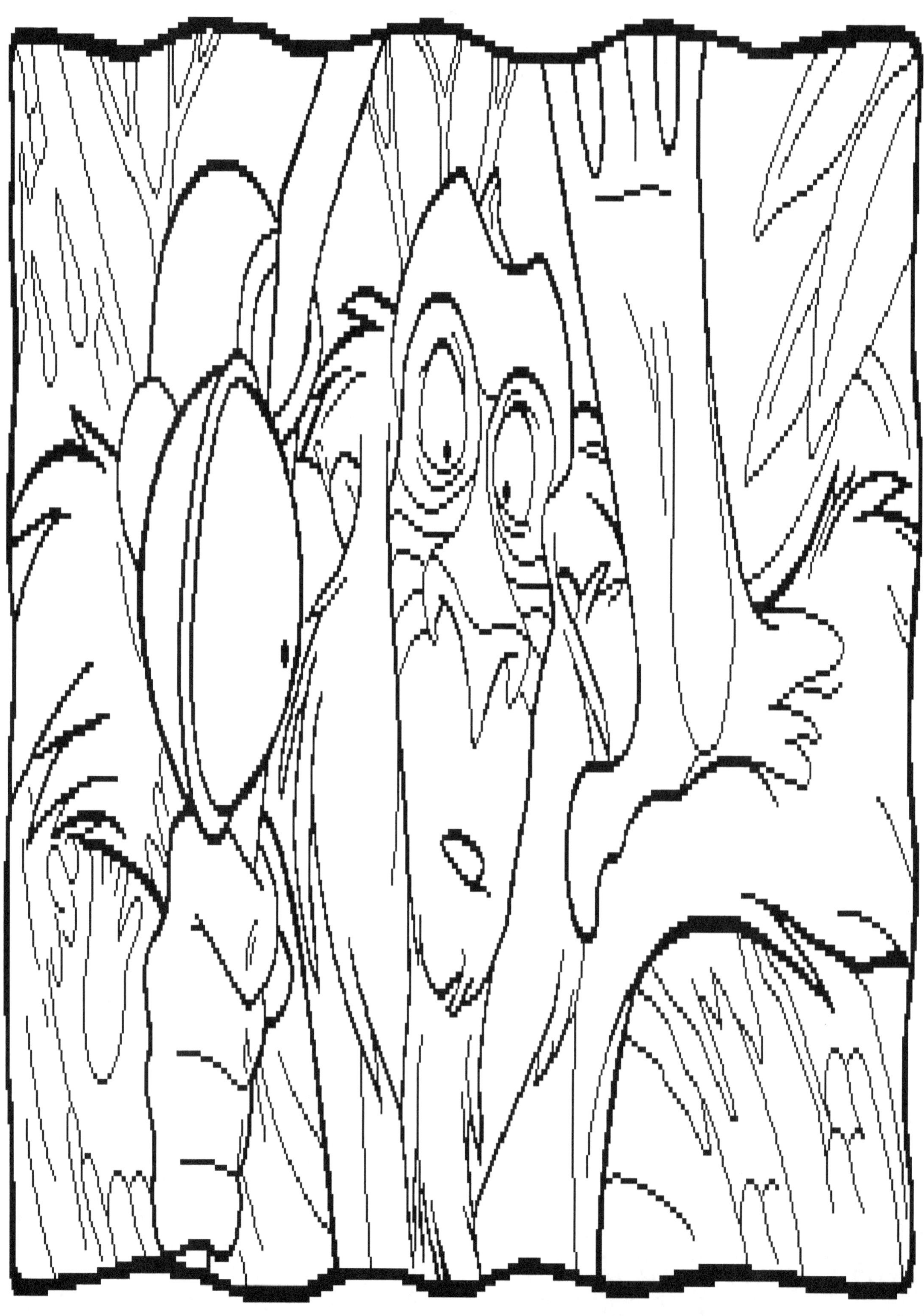

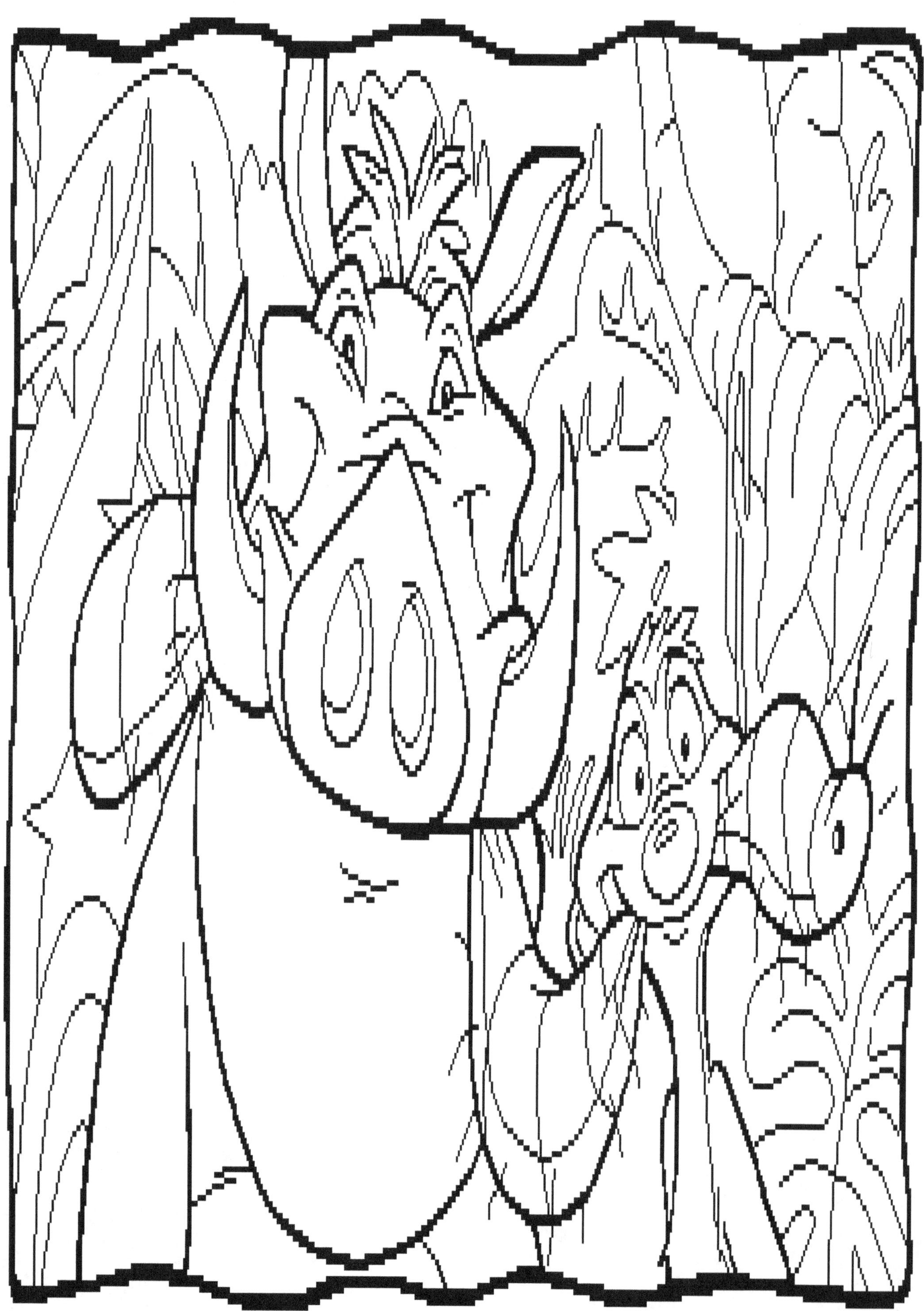

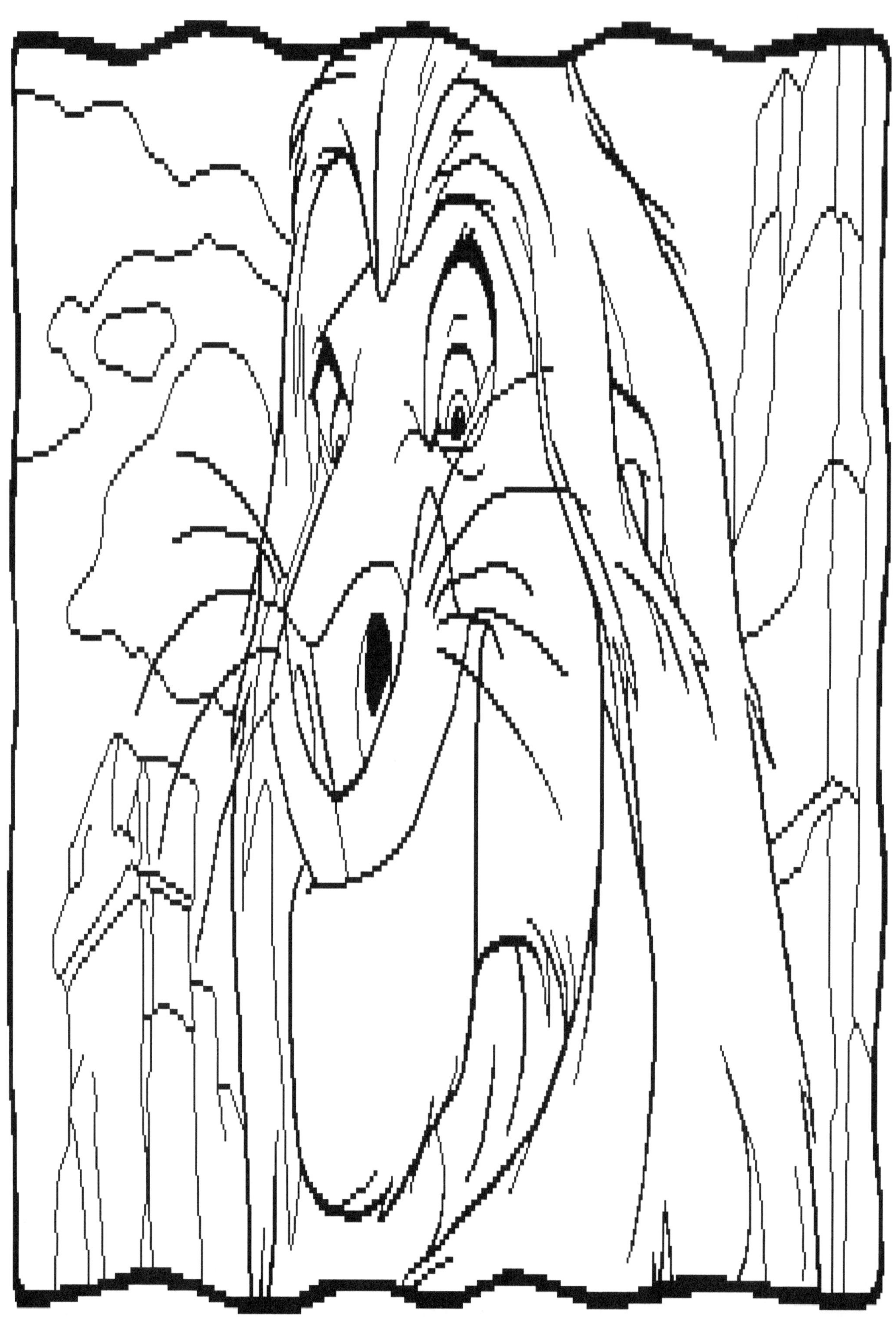

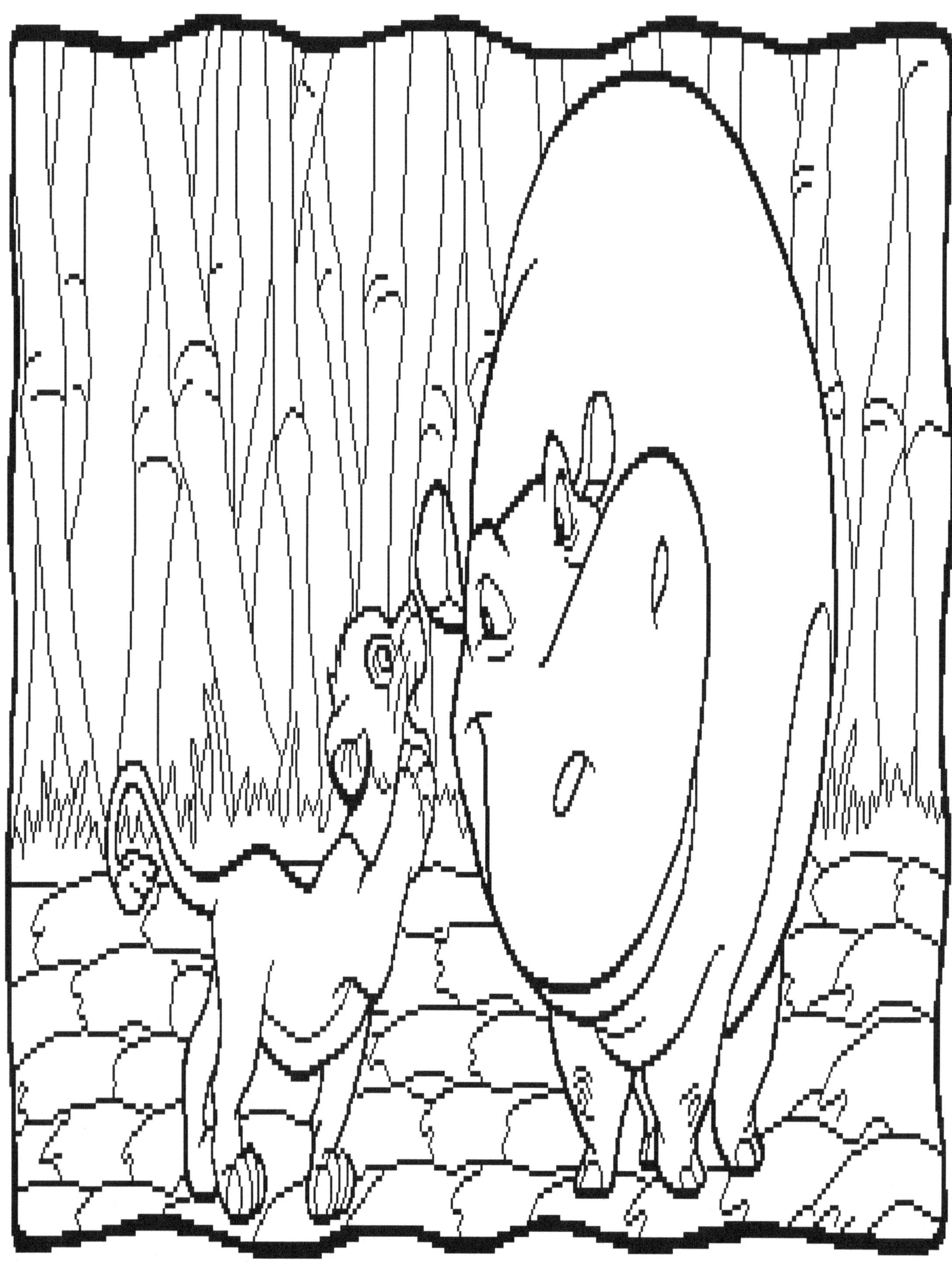

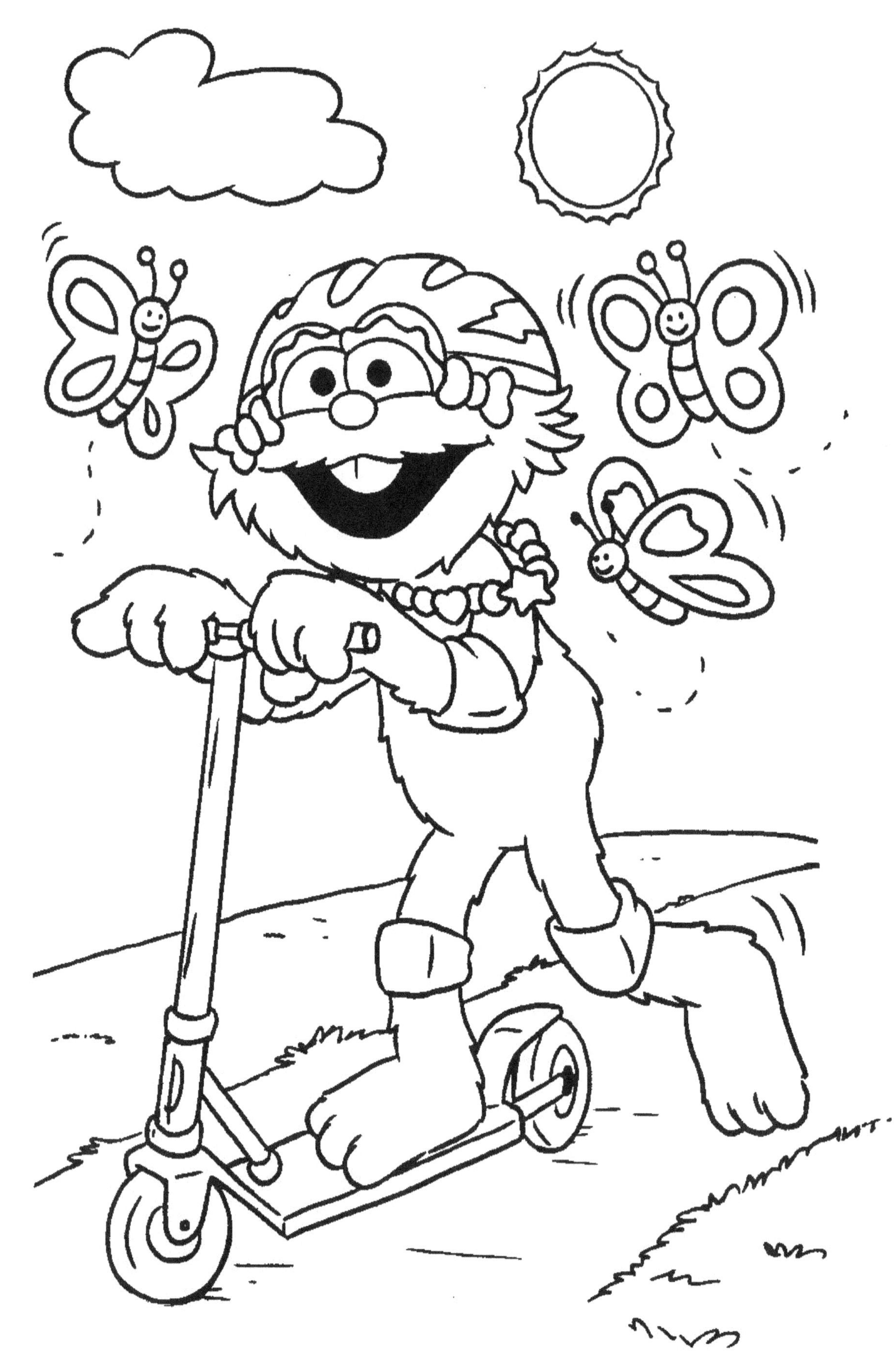

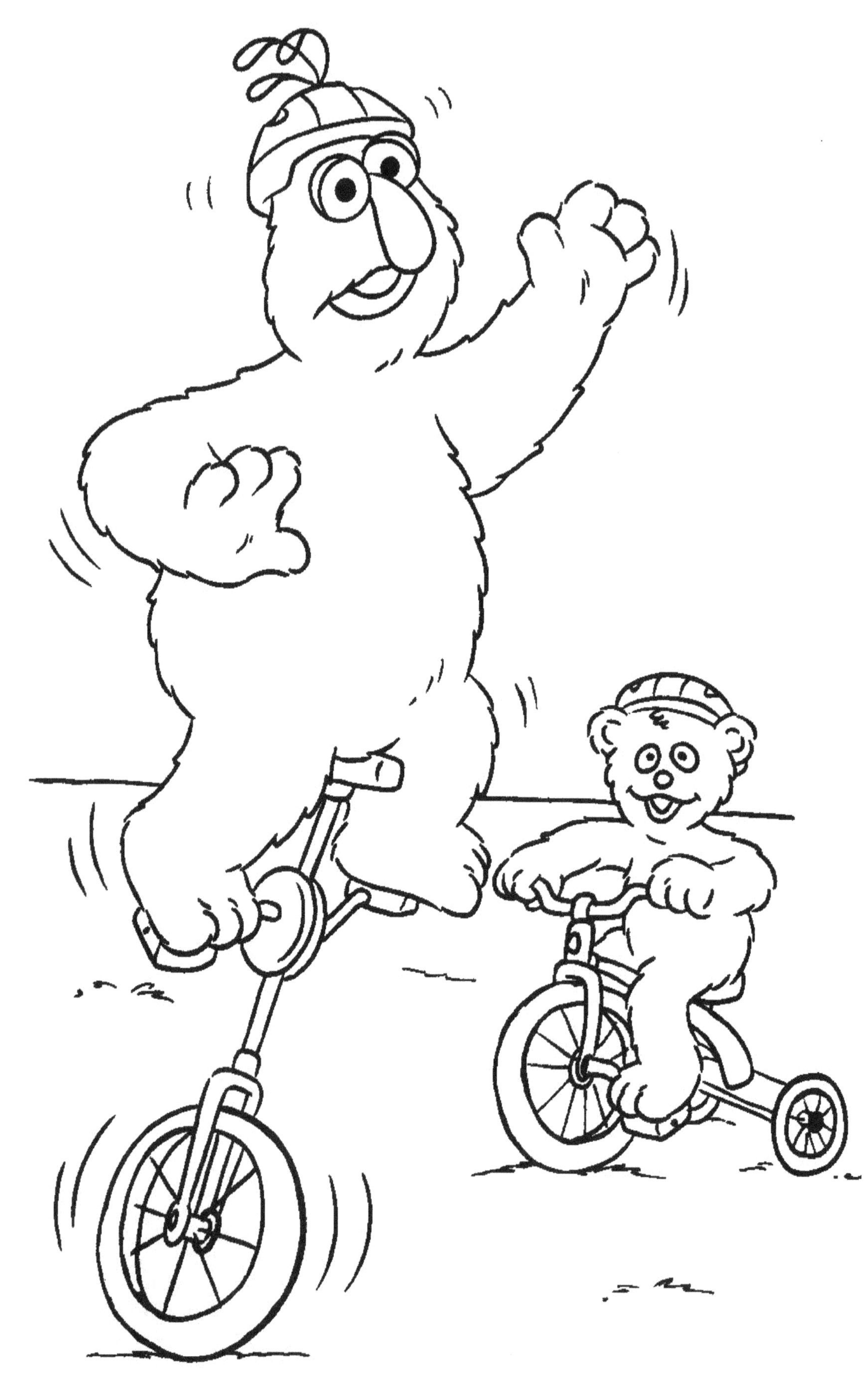

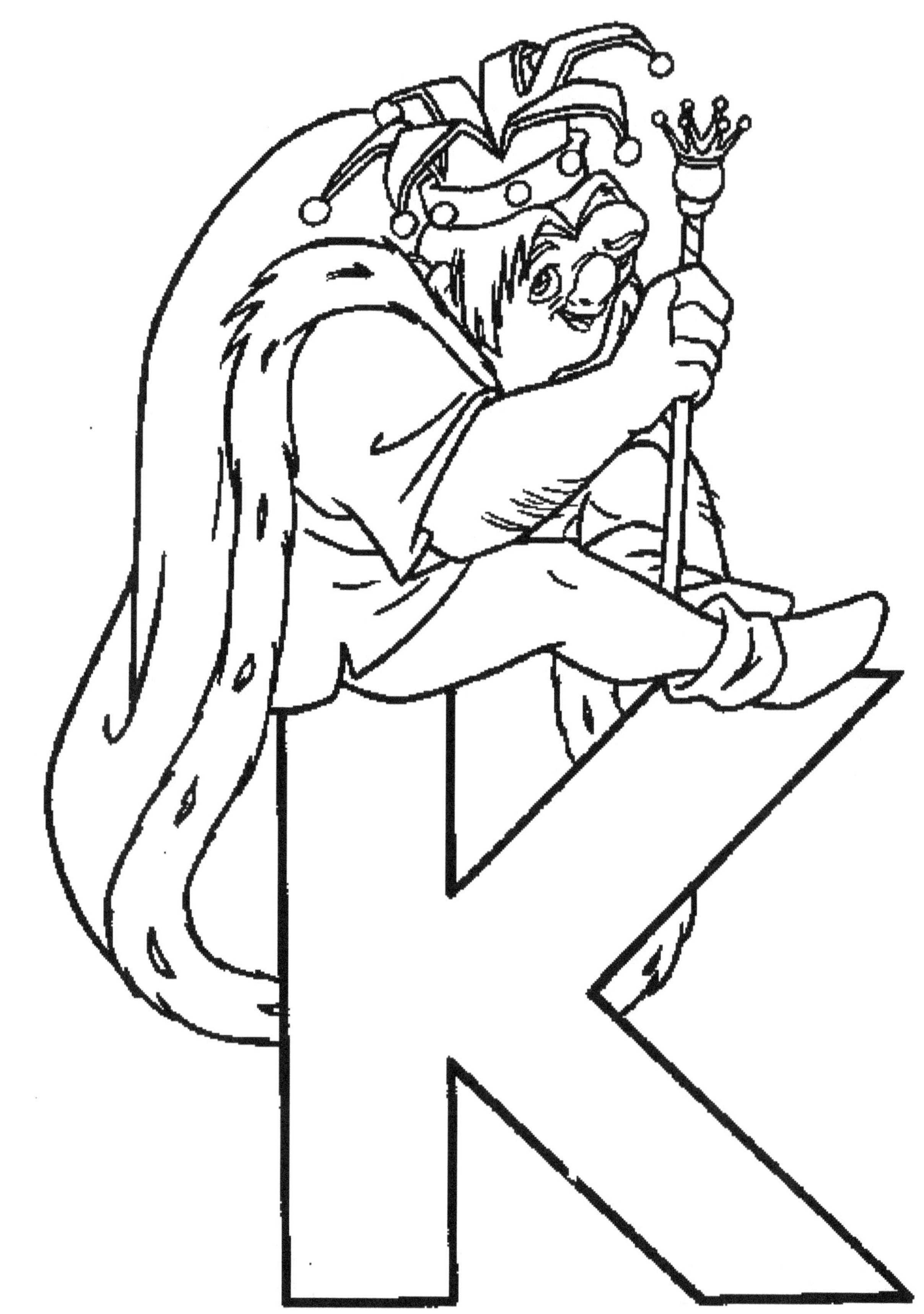

K

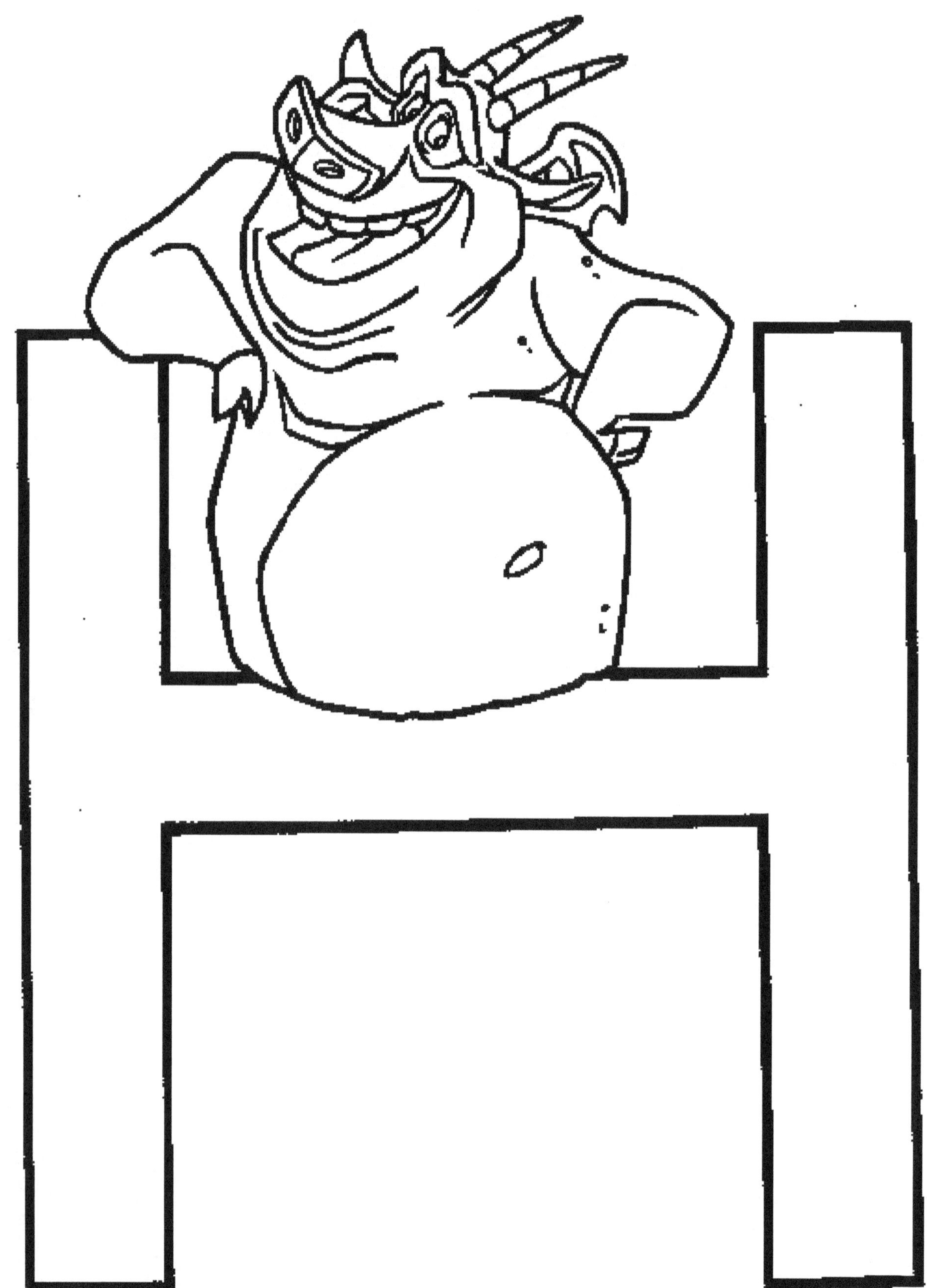

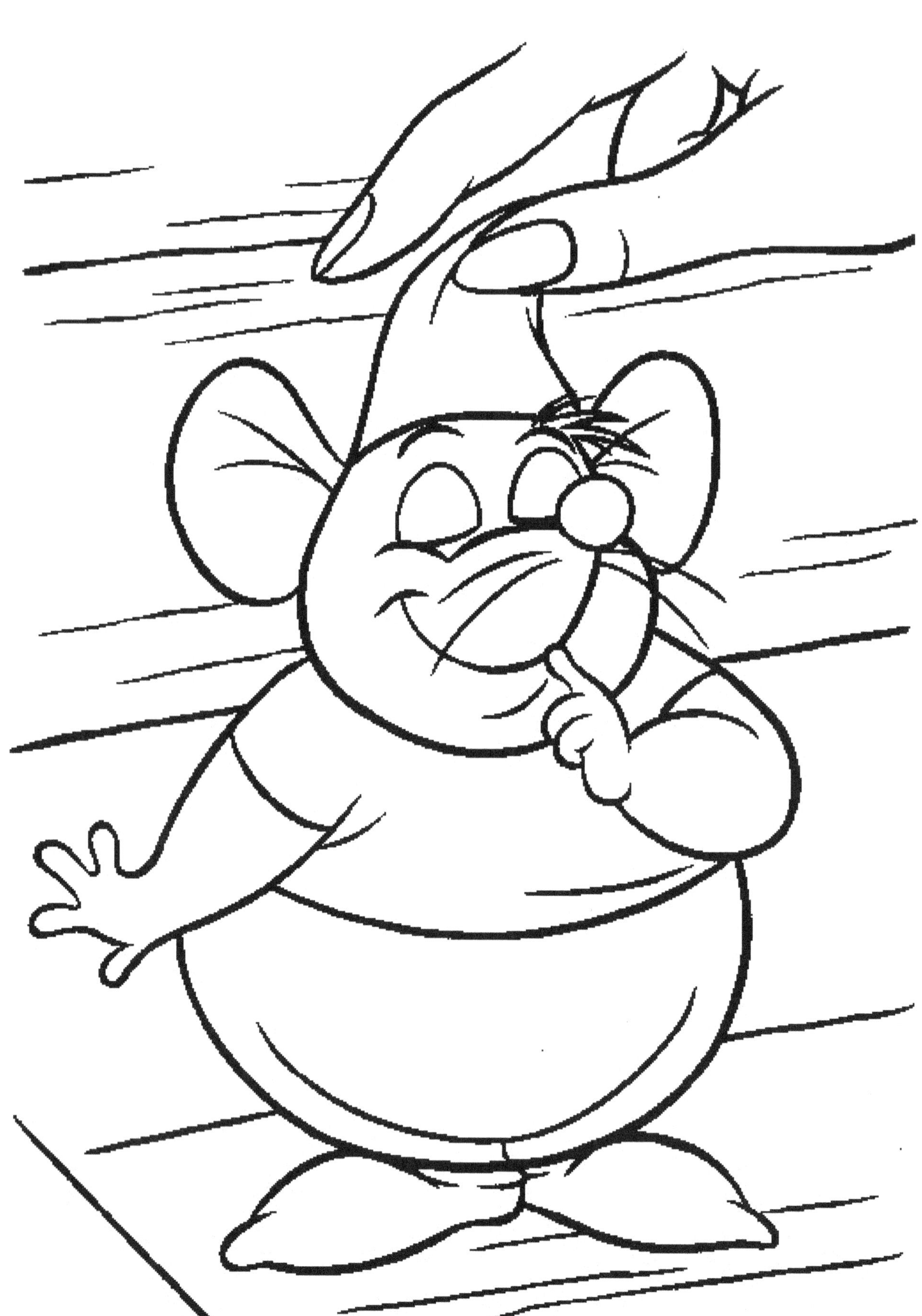

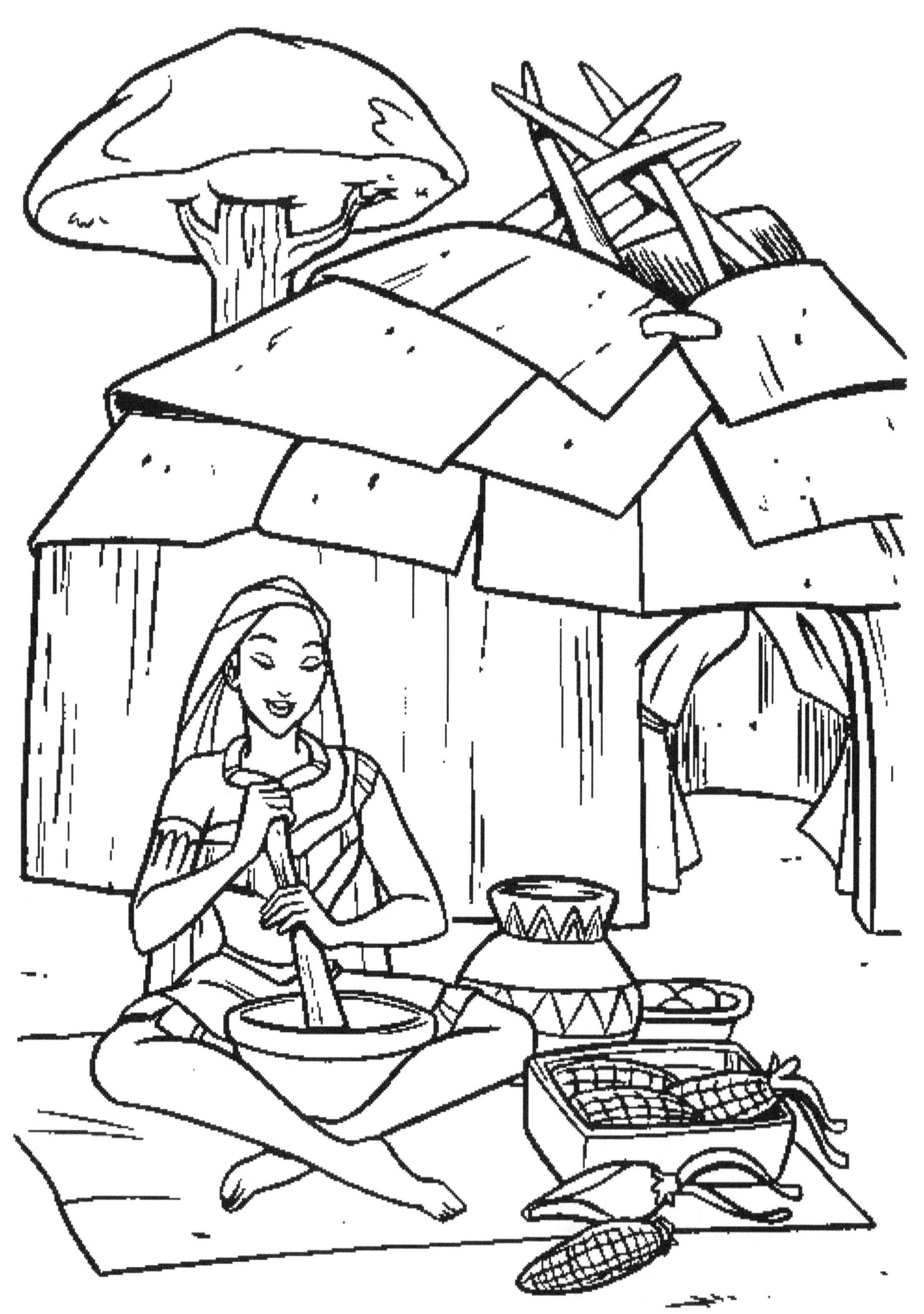

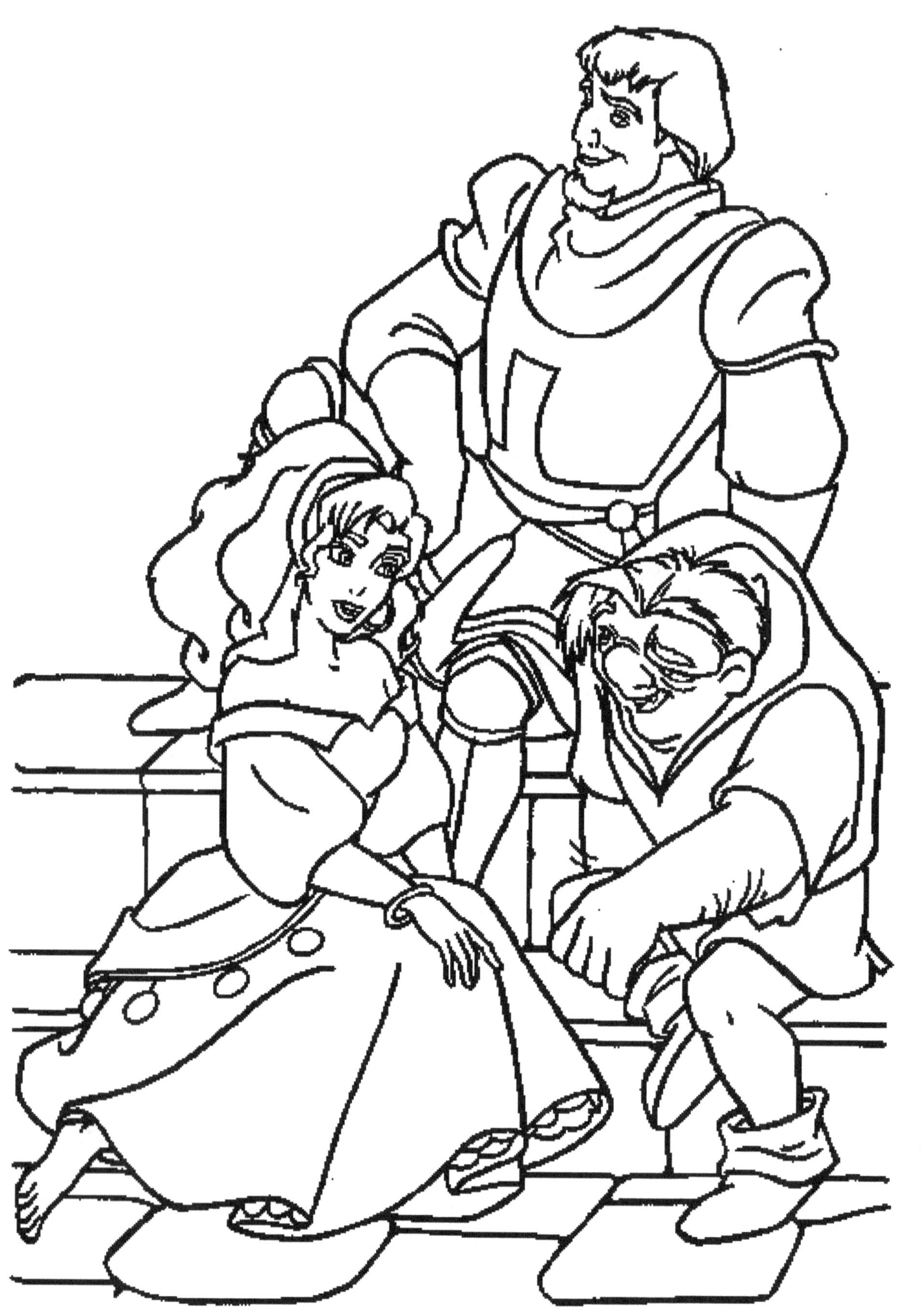

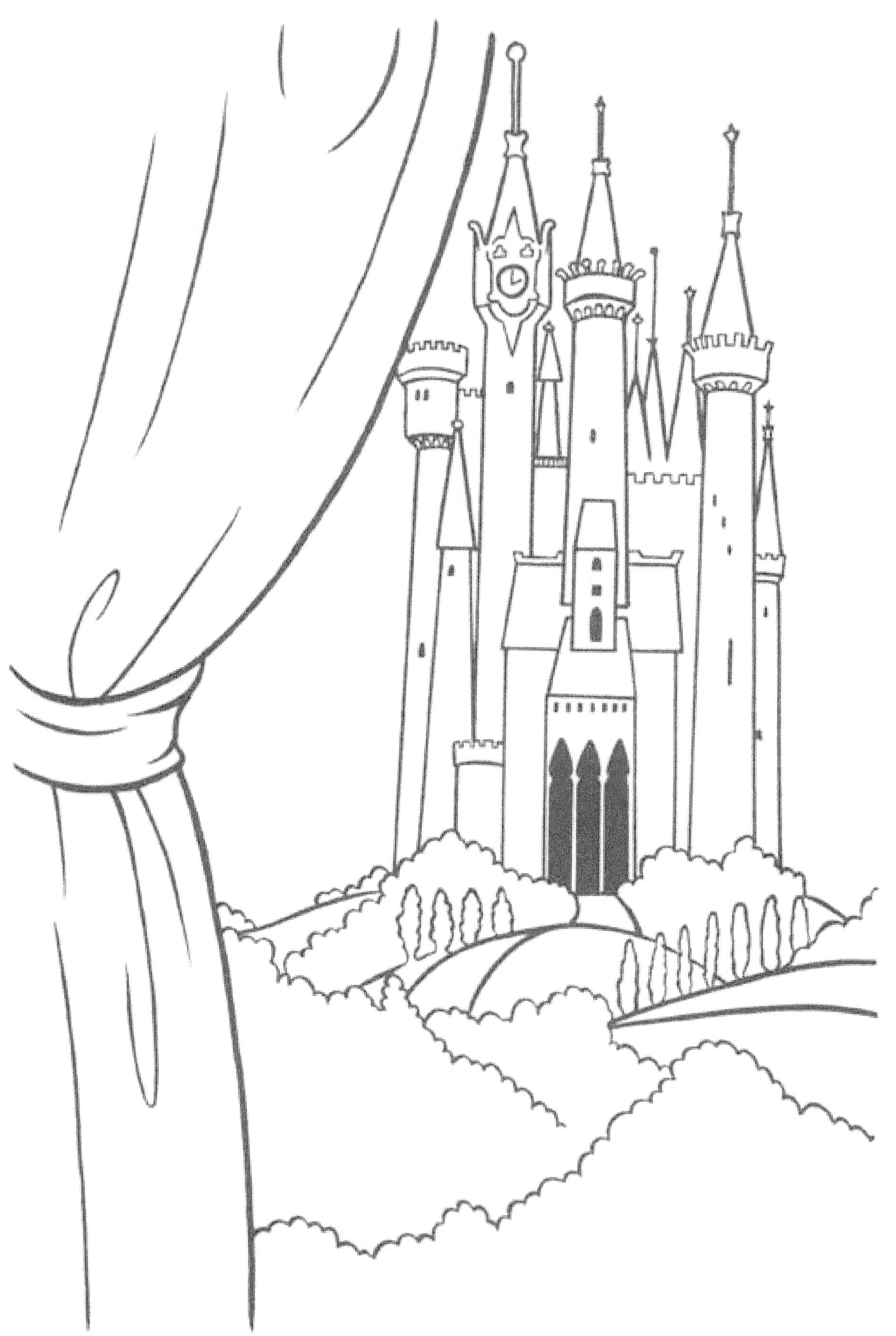

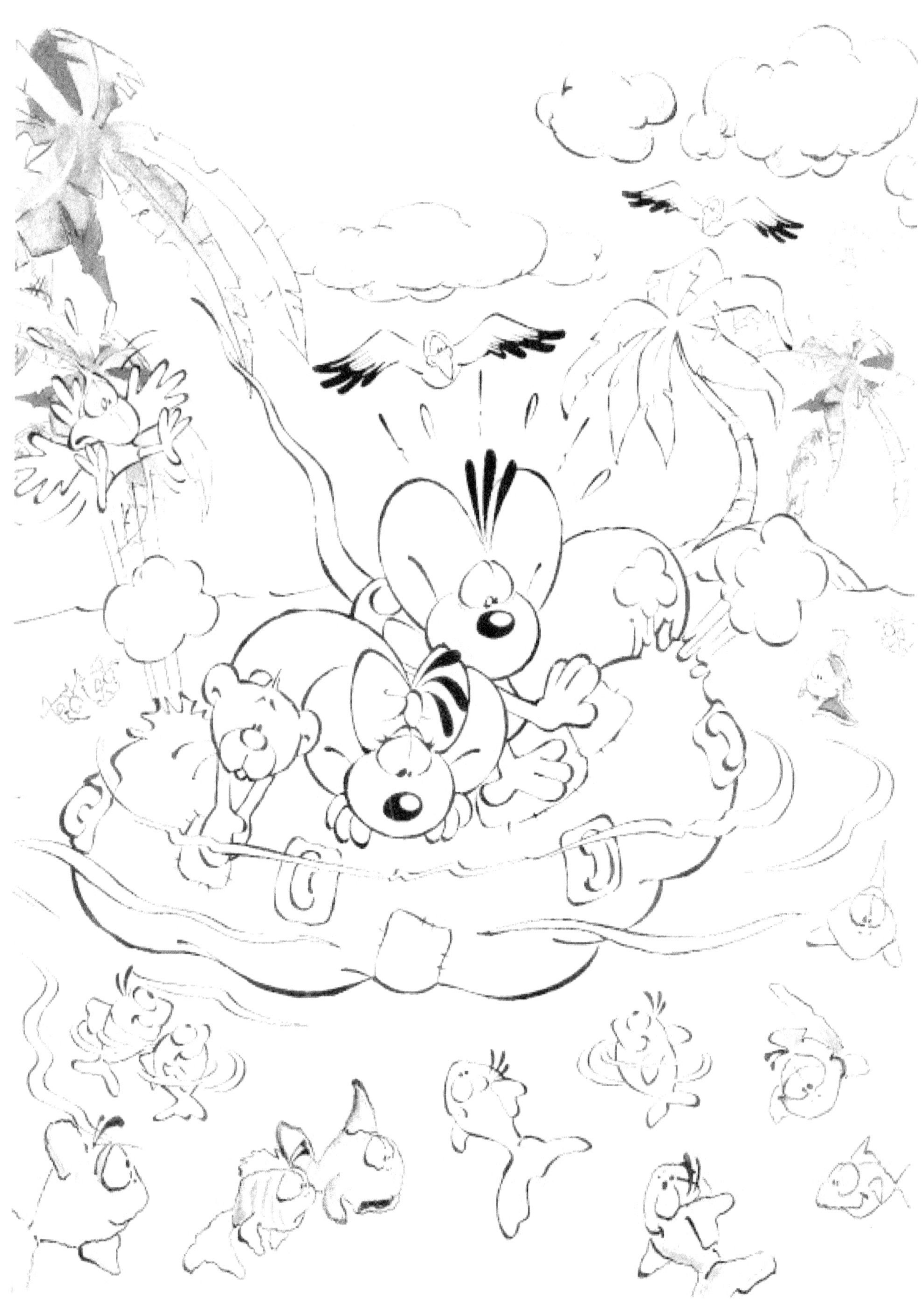

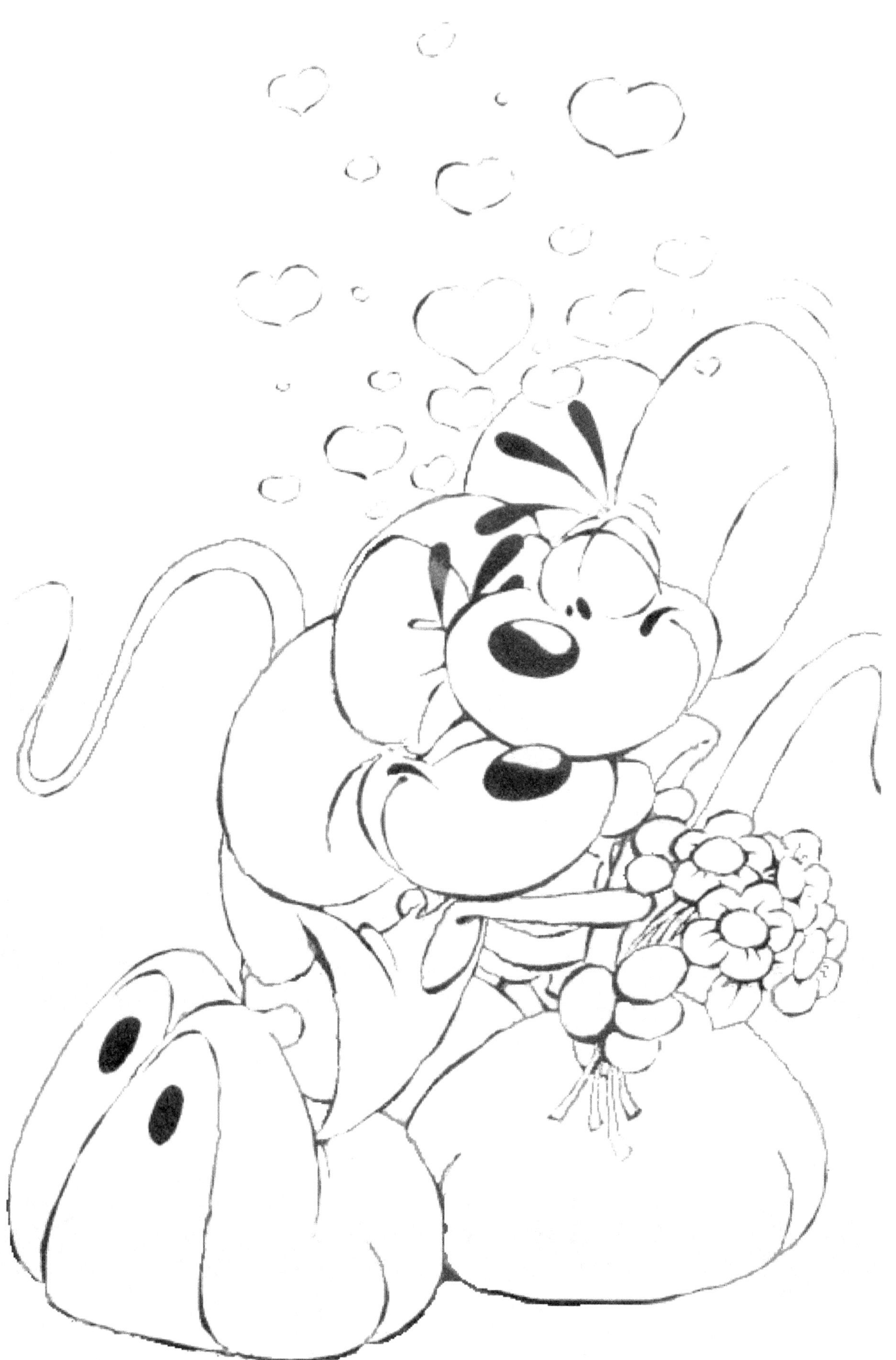

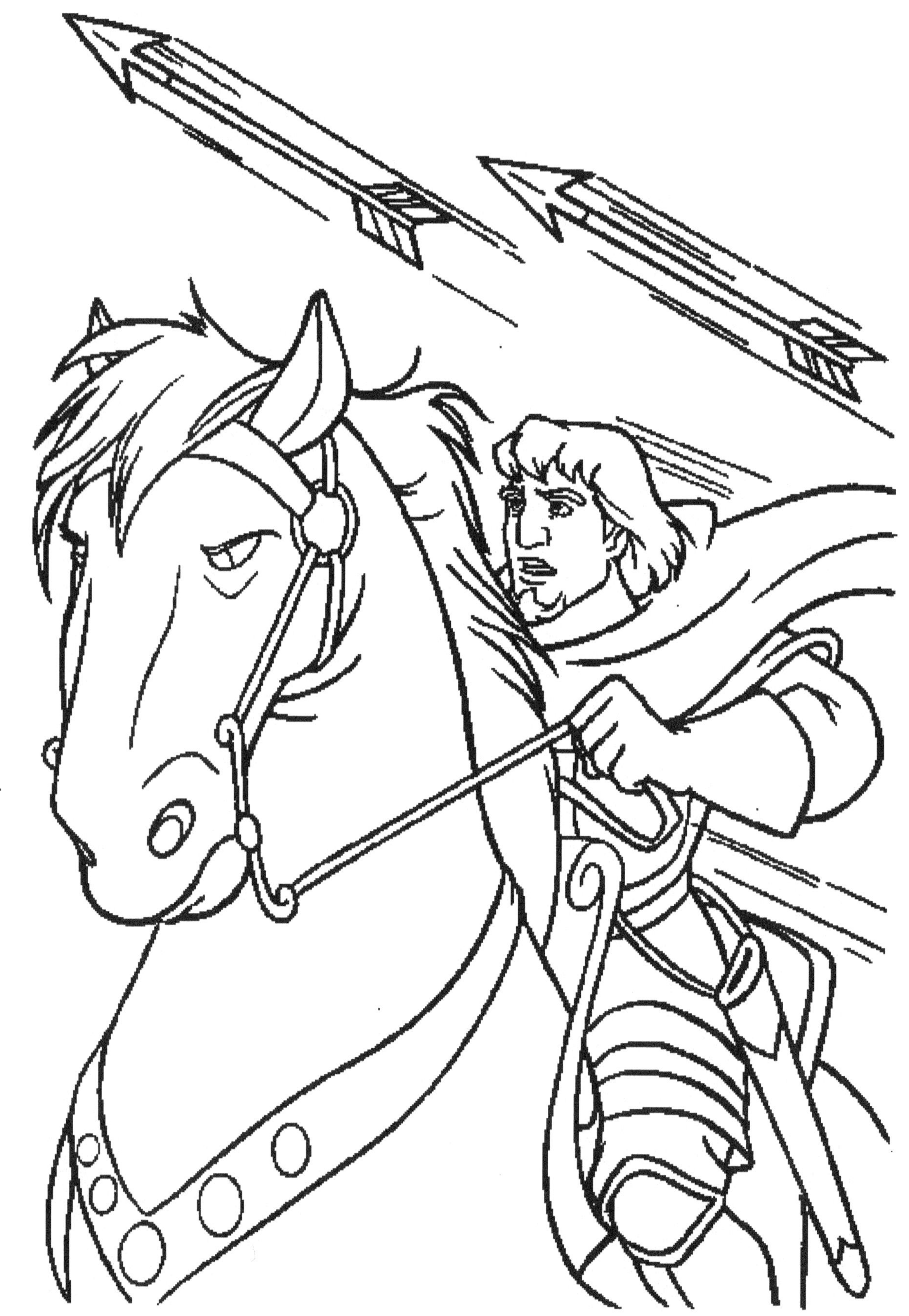

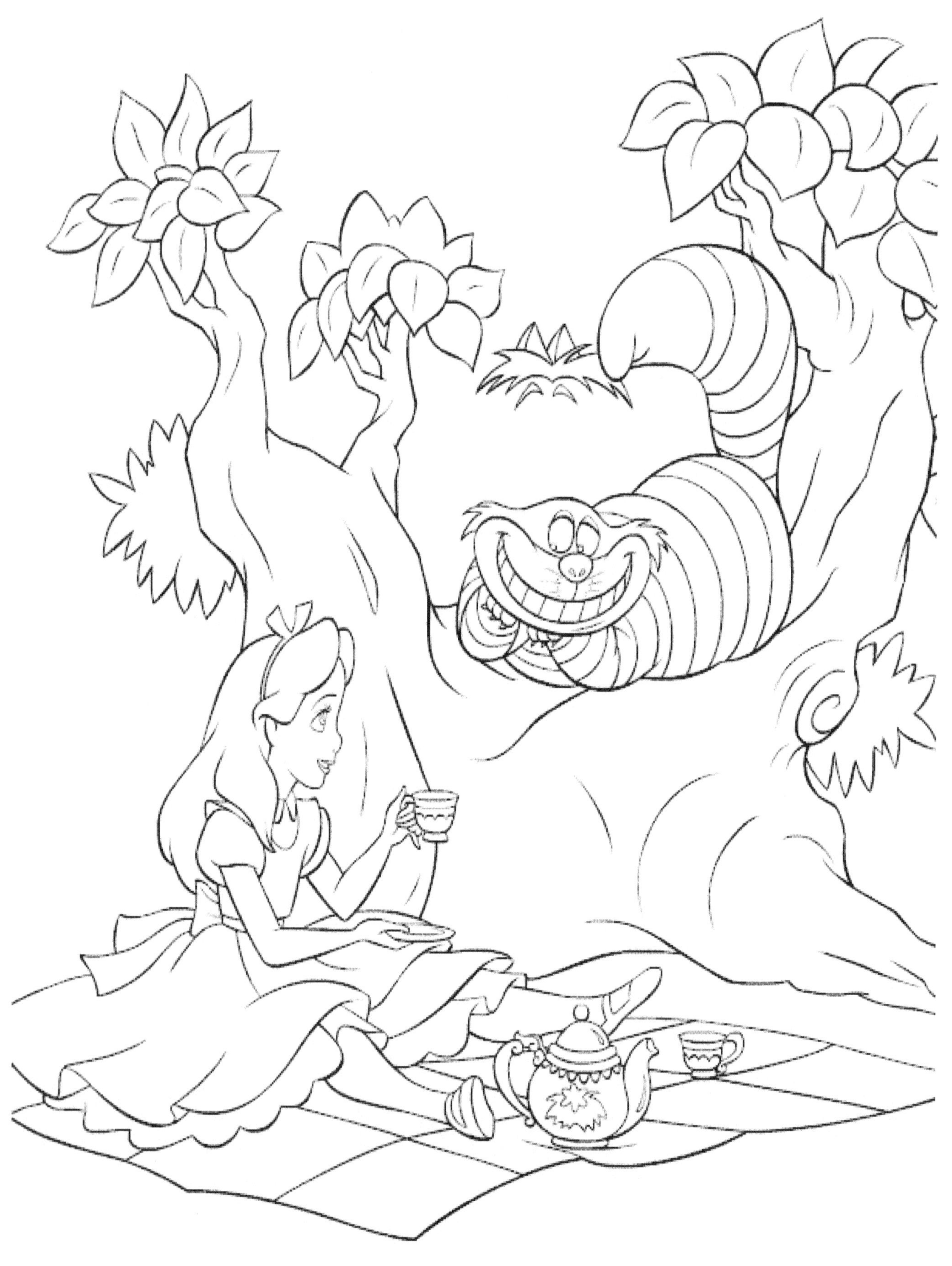

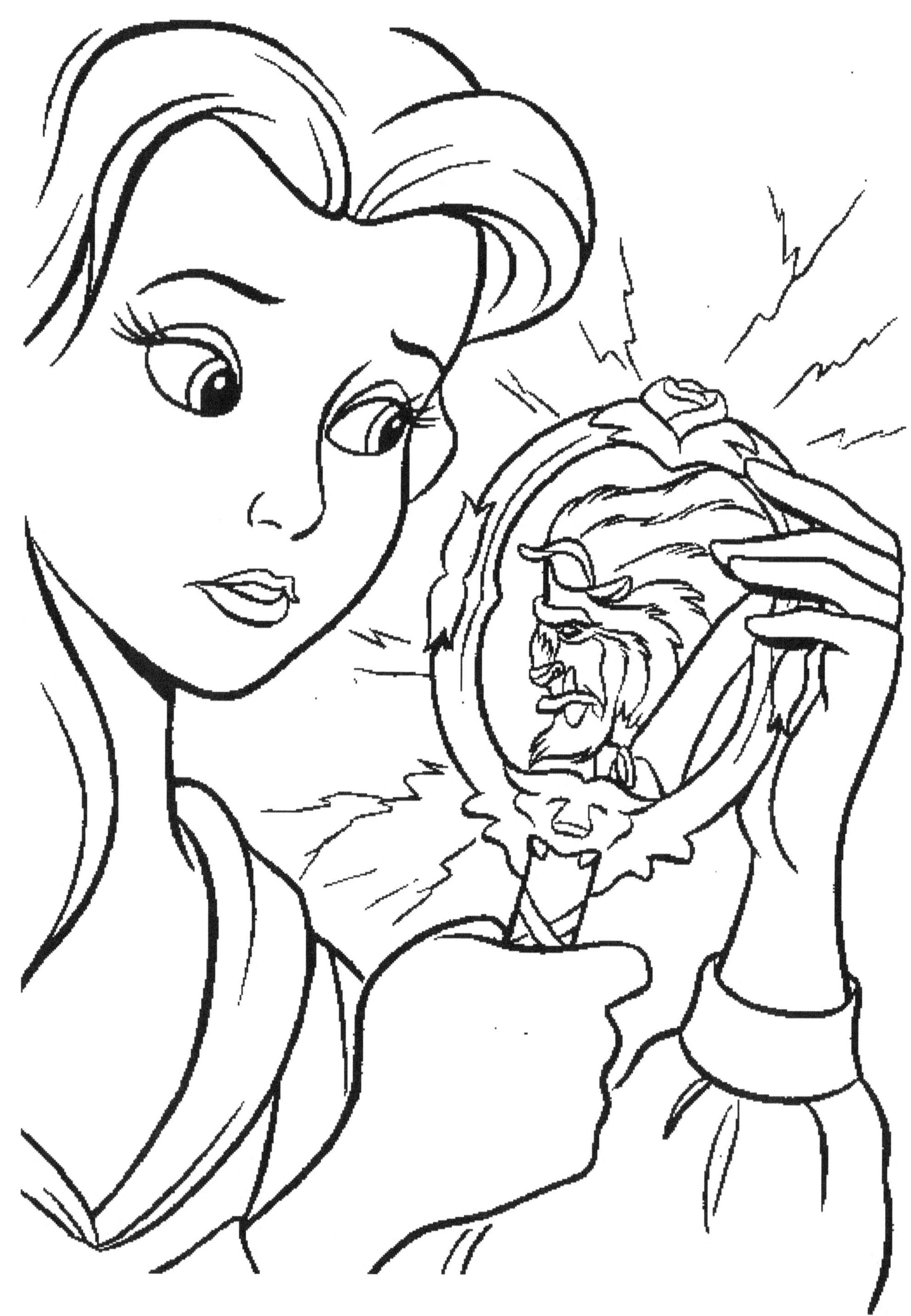

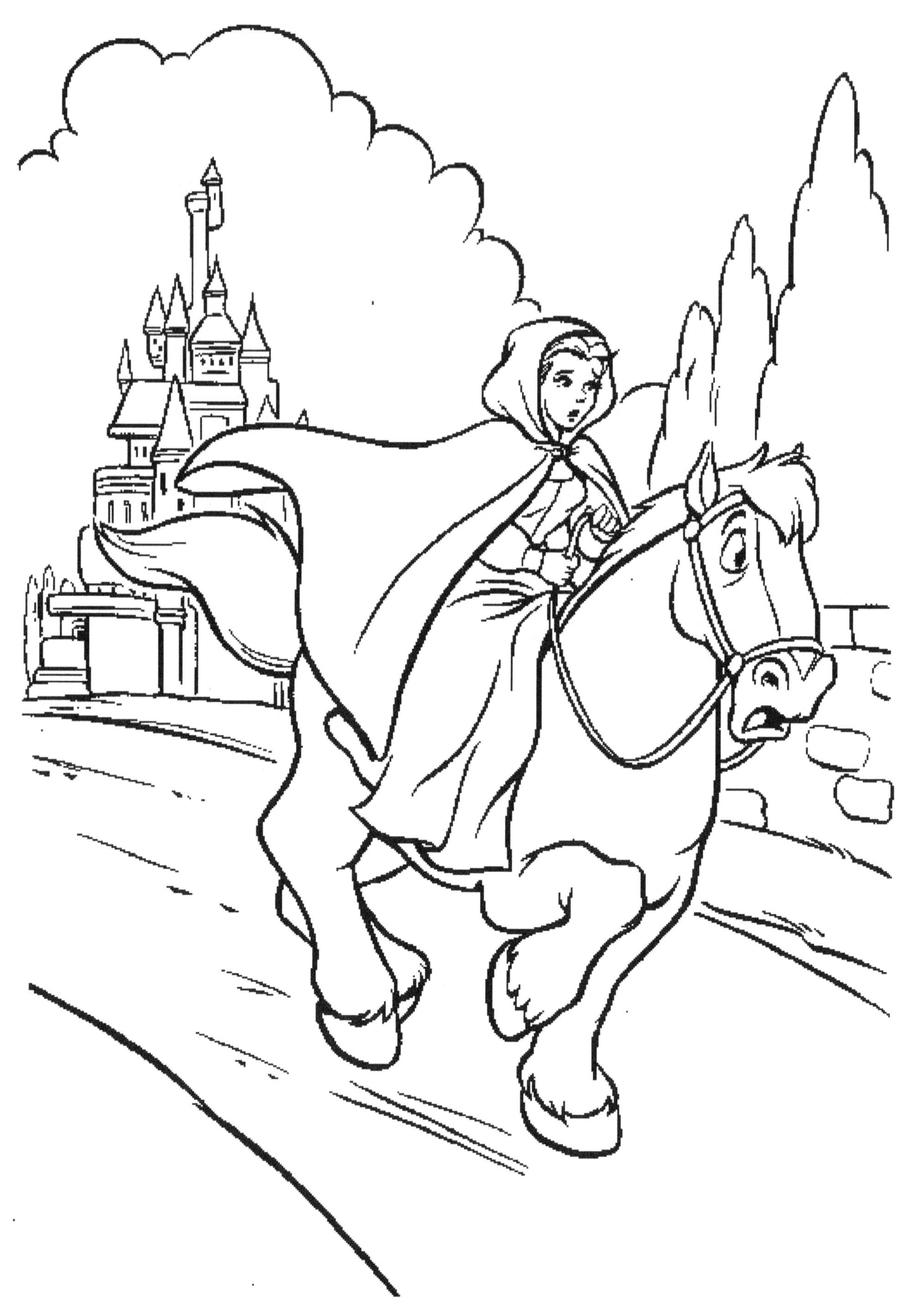

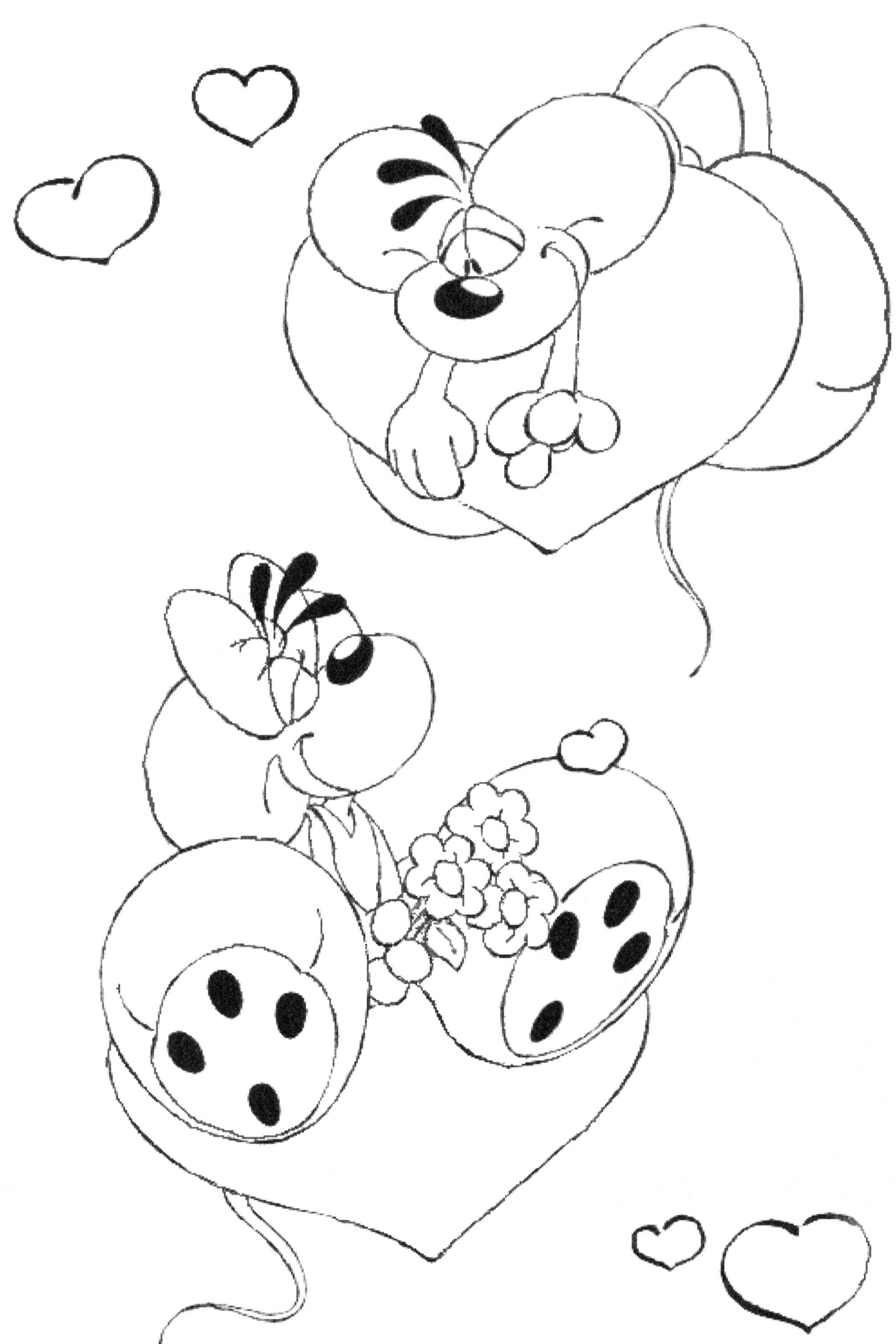

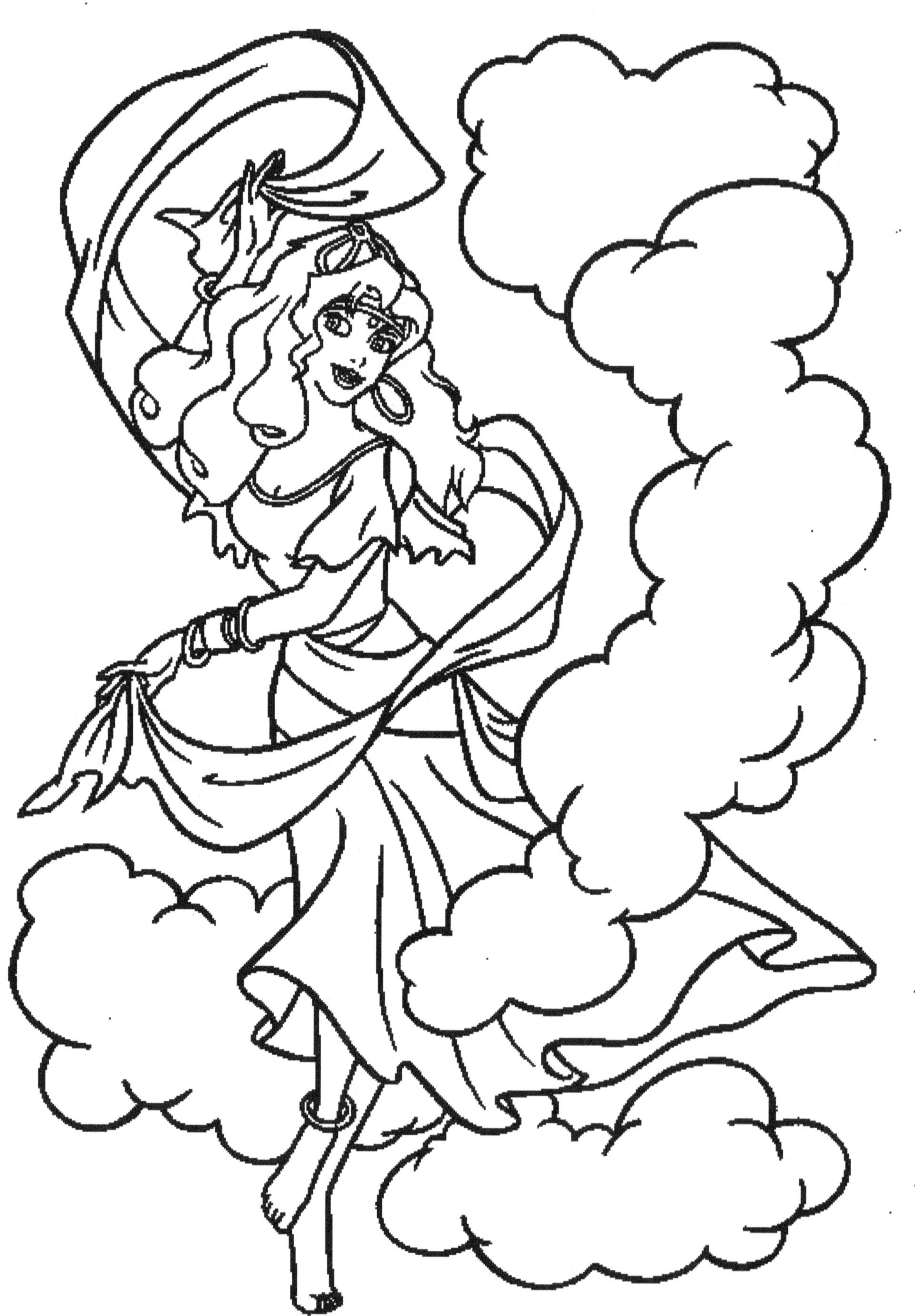

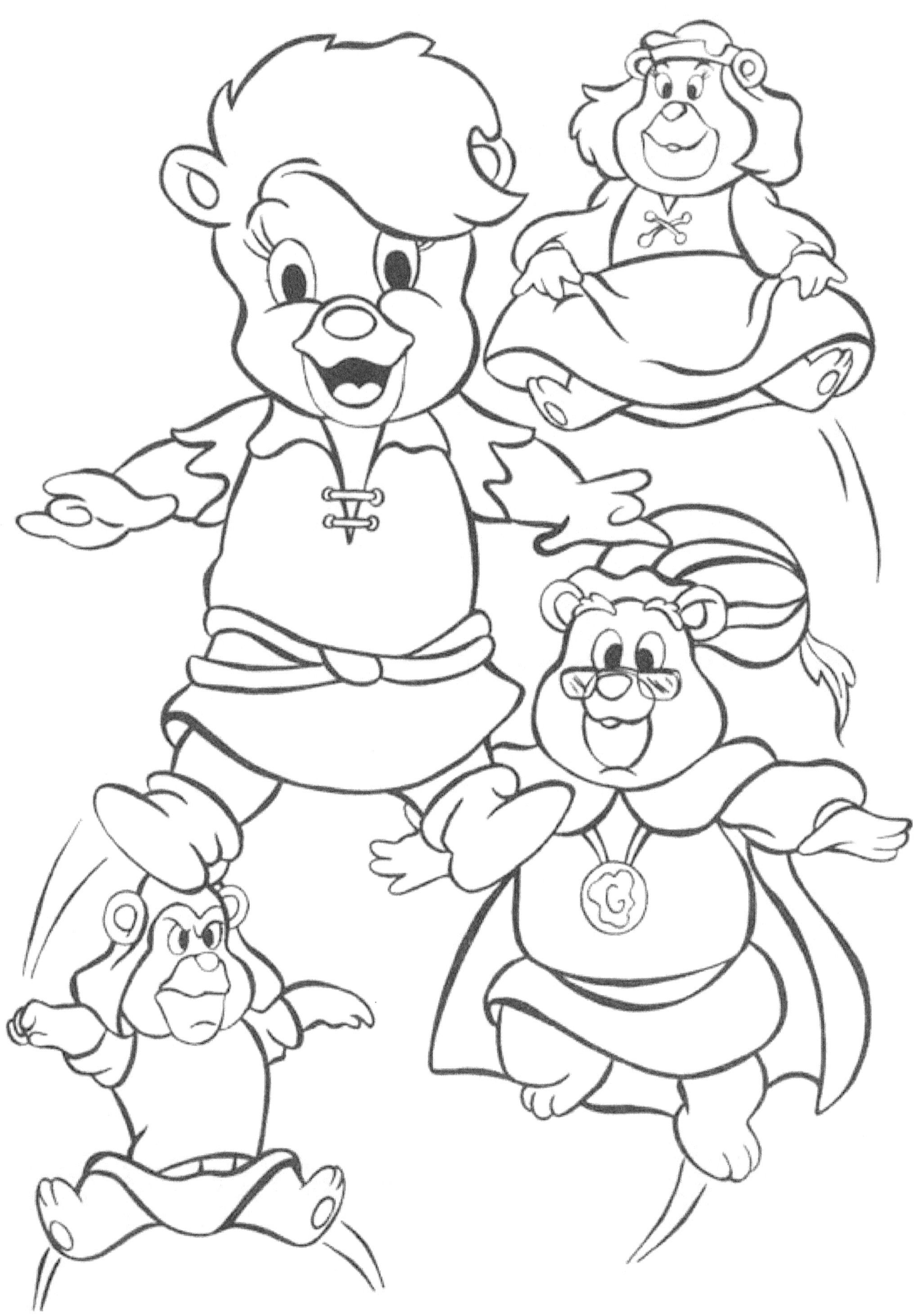

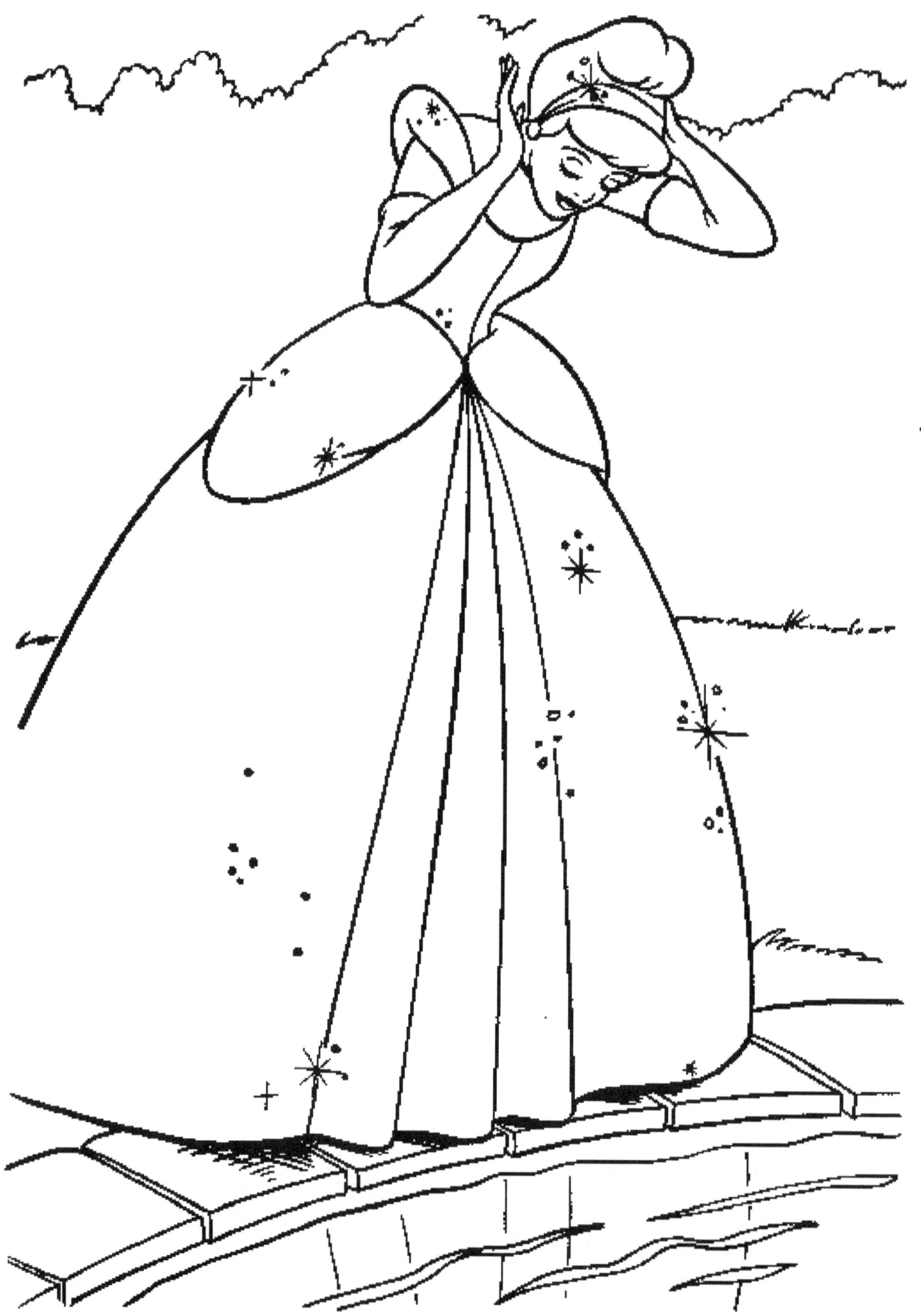

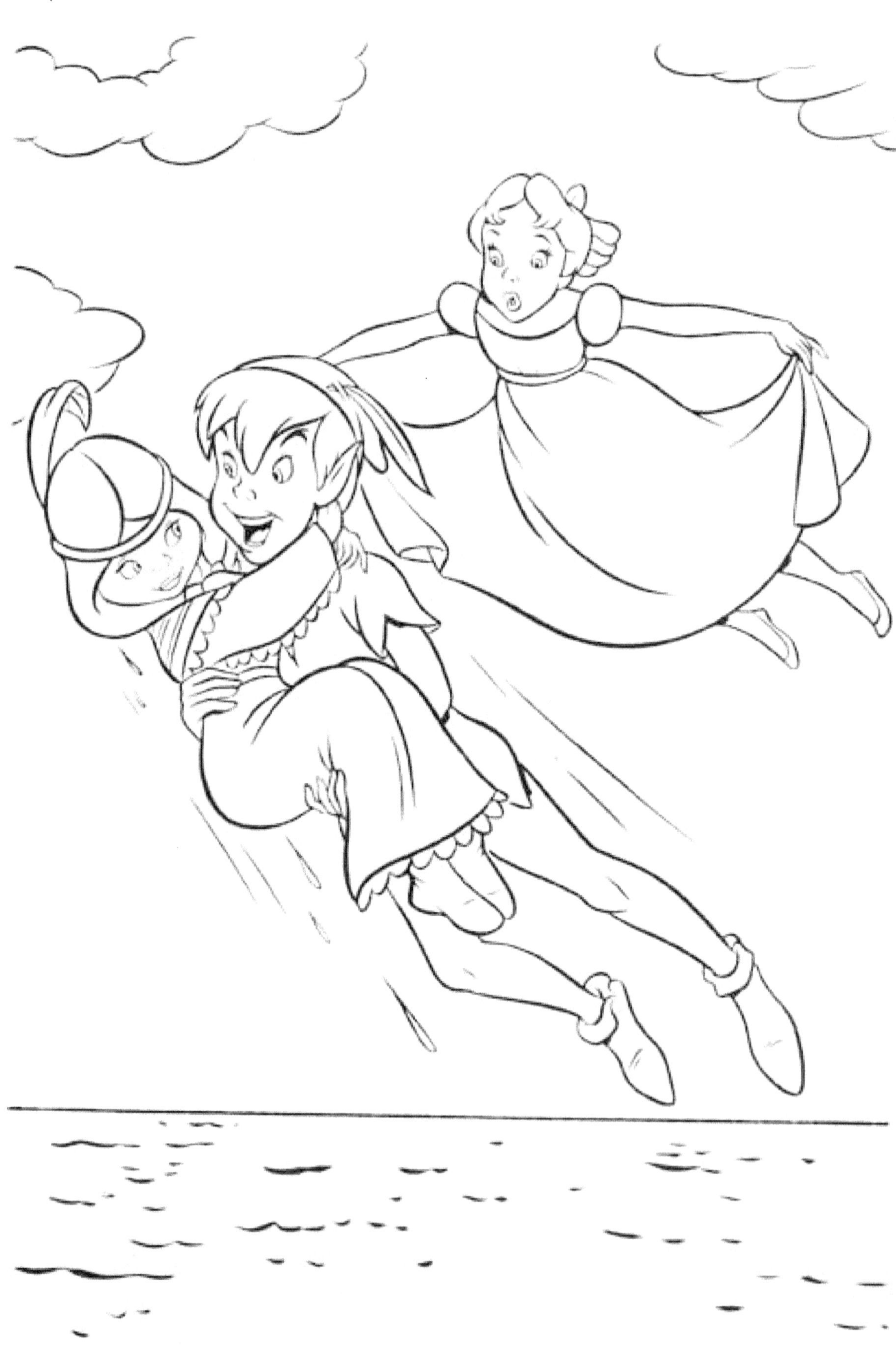

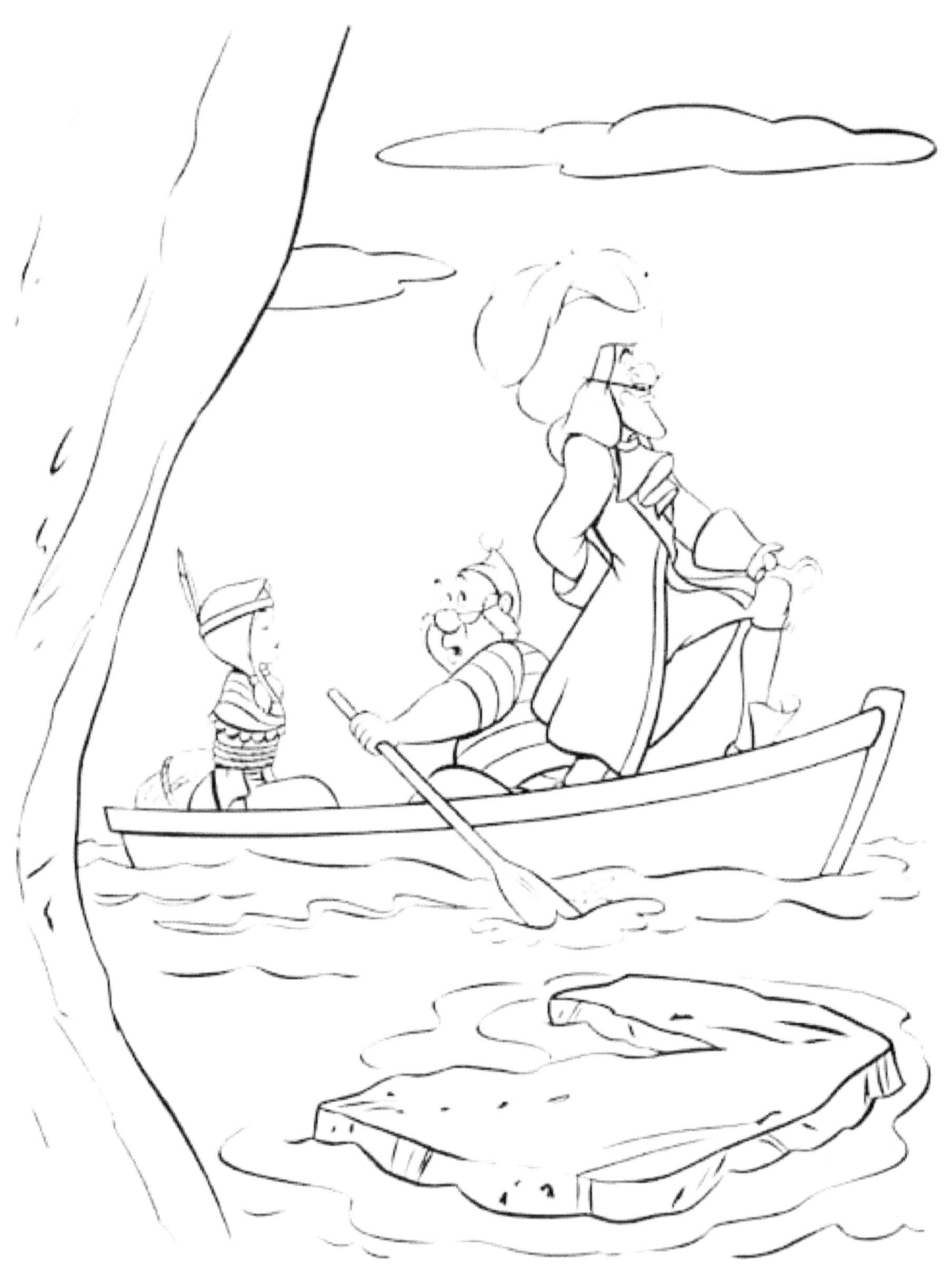

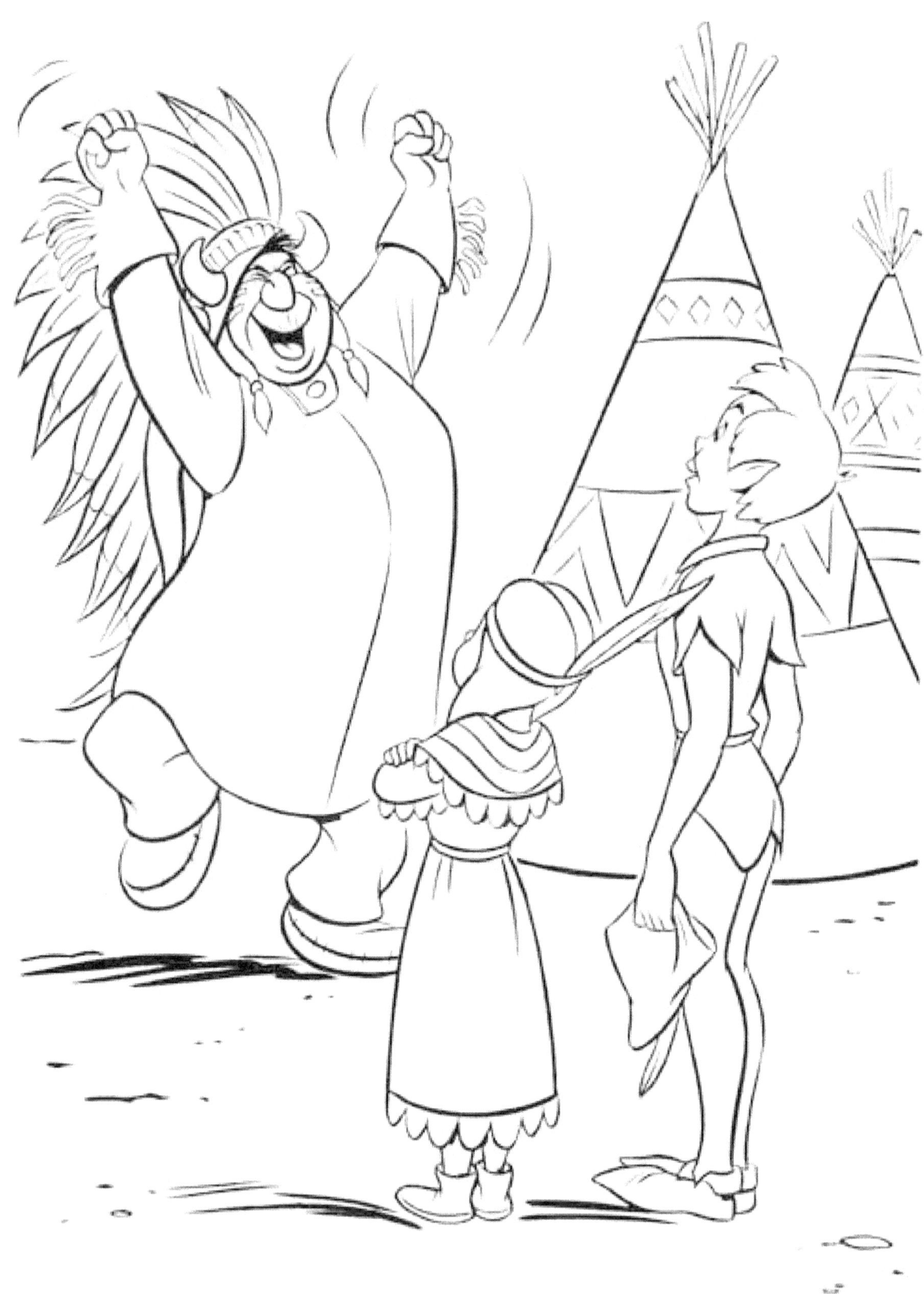

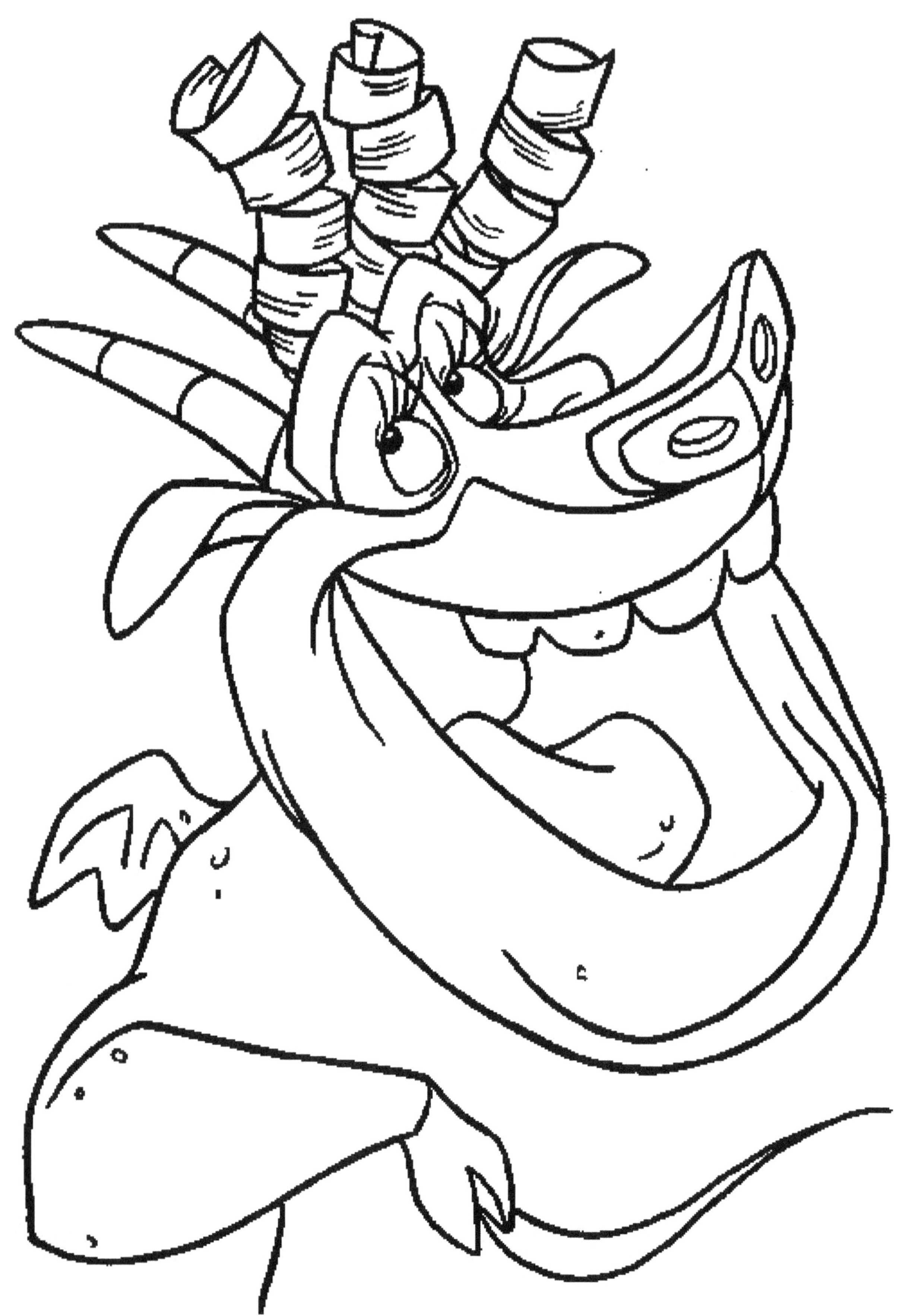

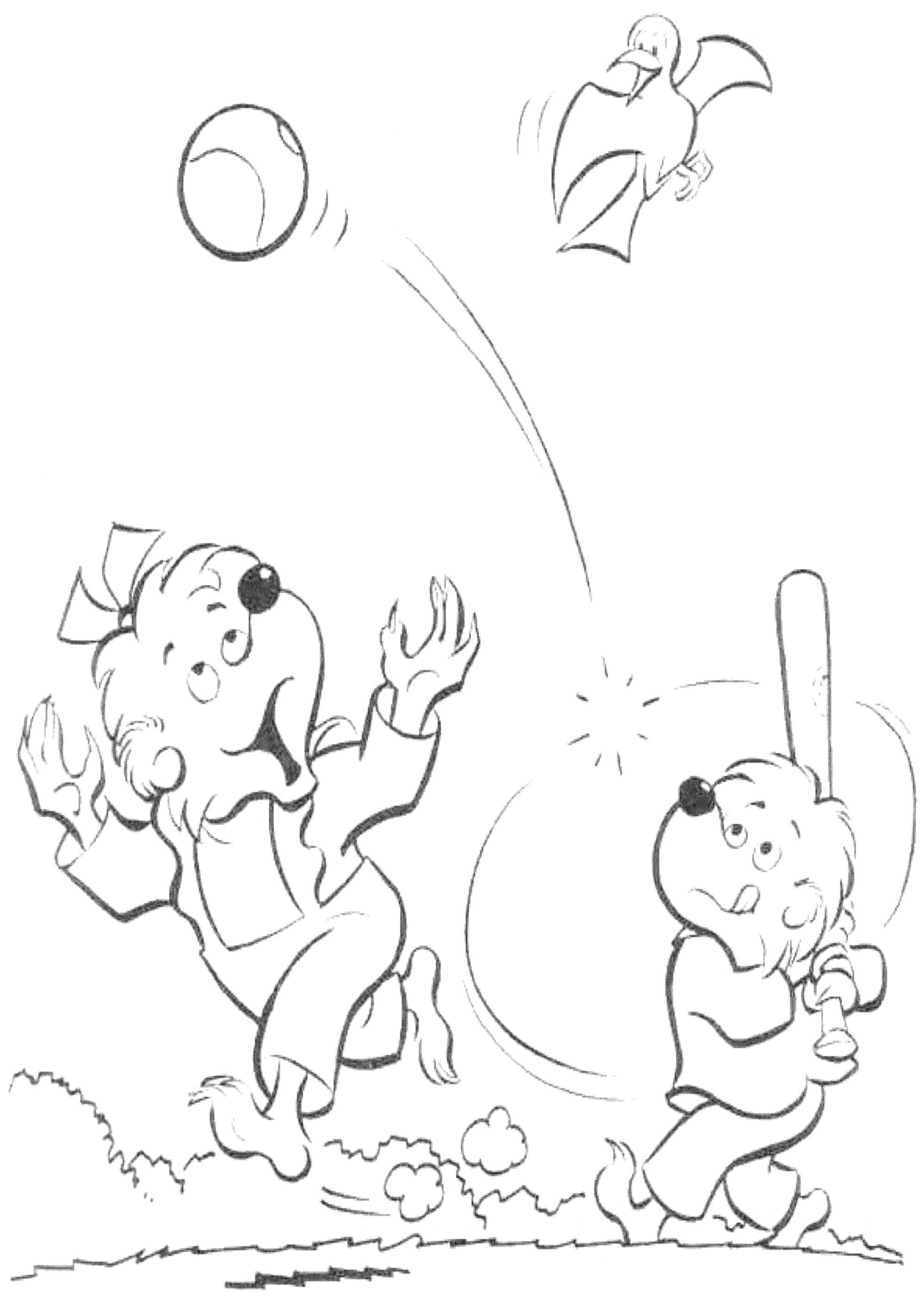

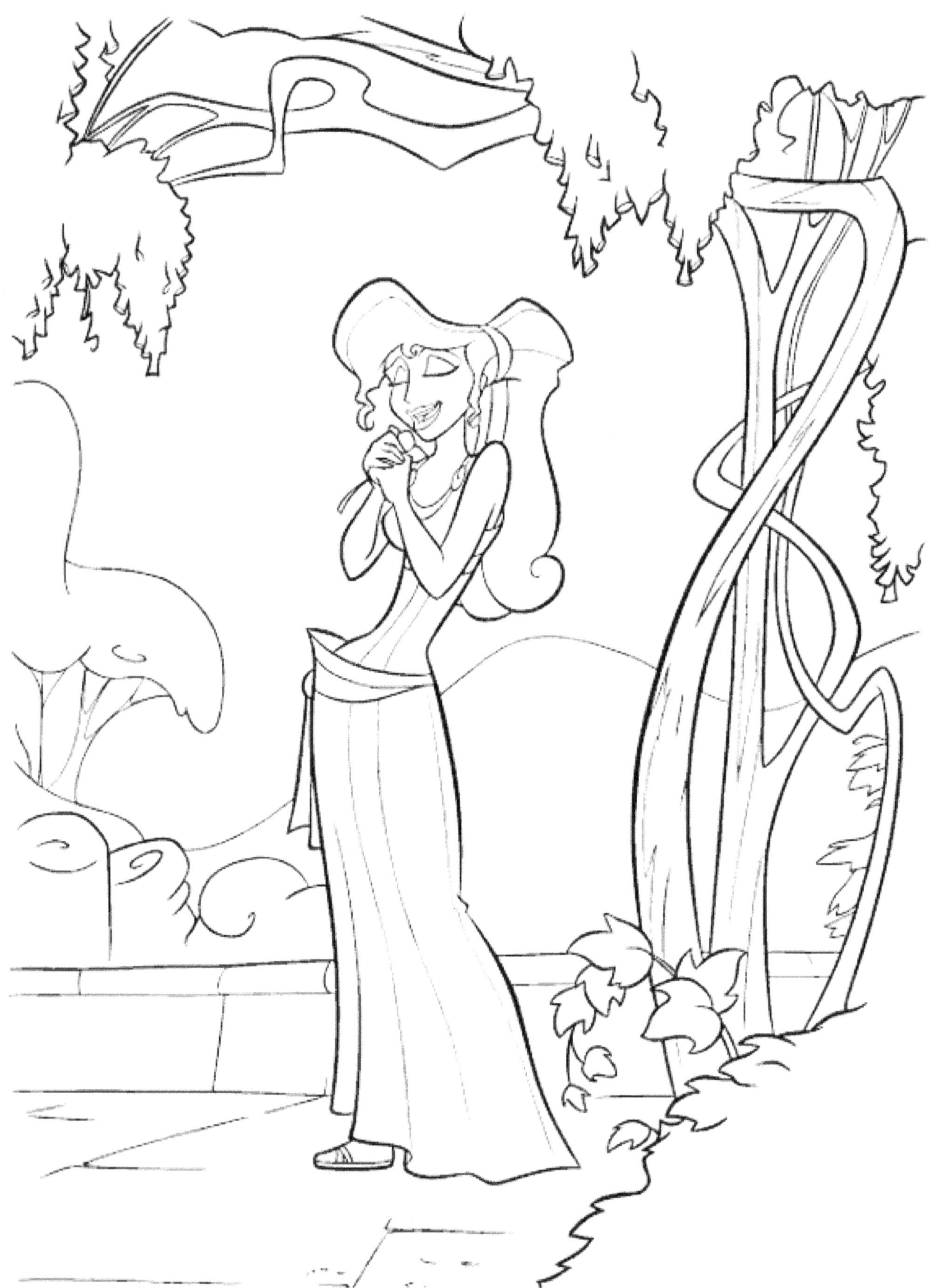

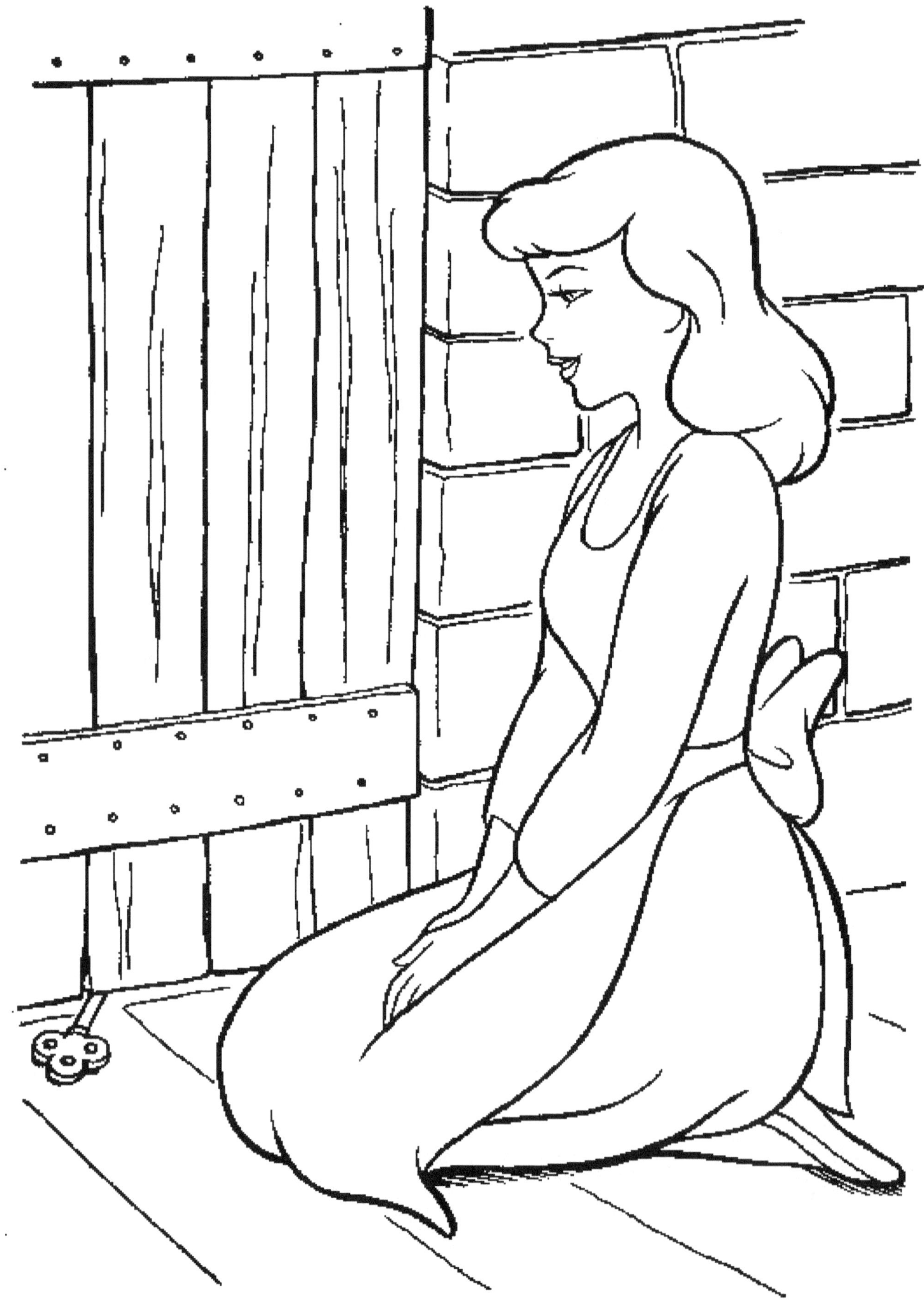

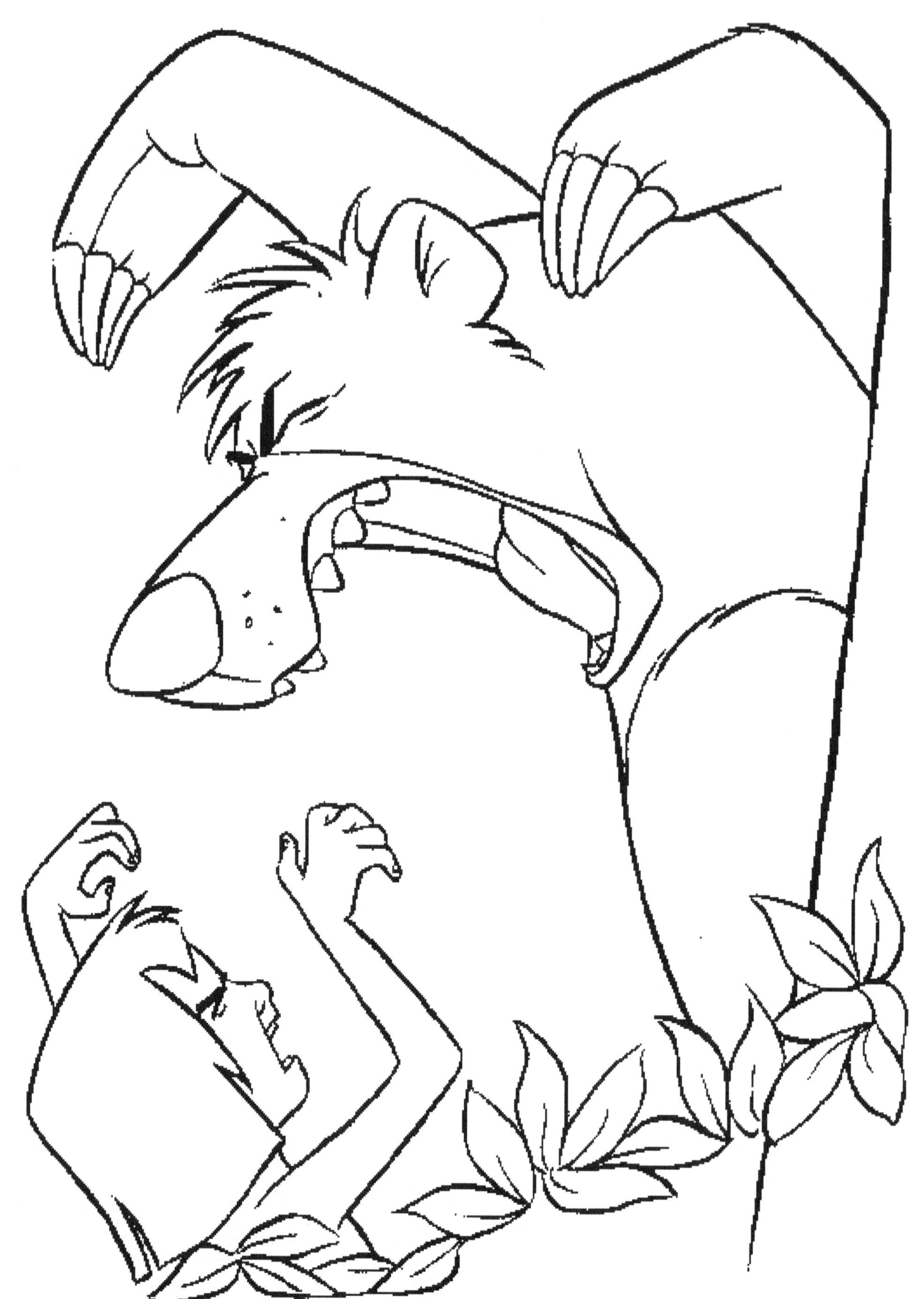

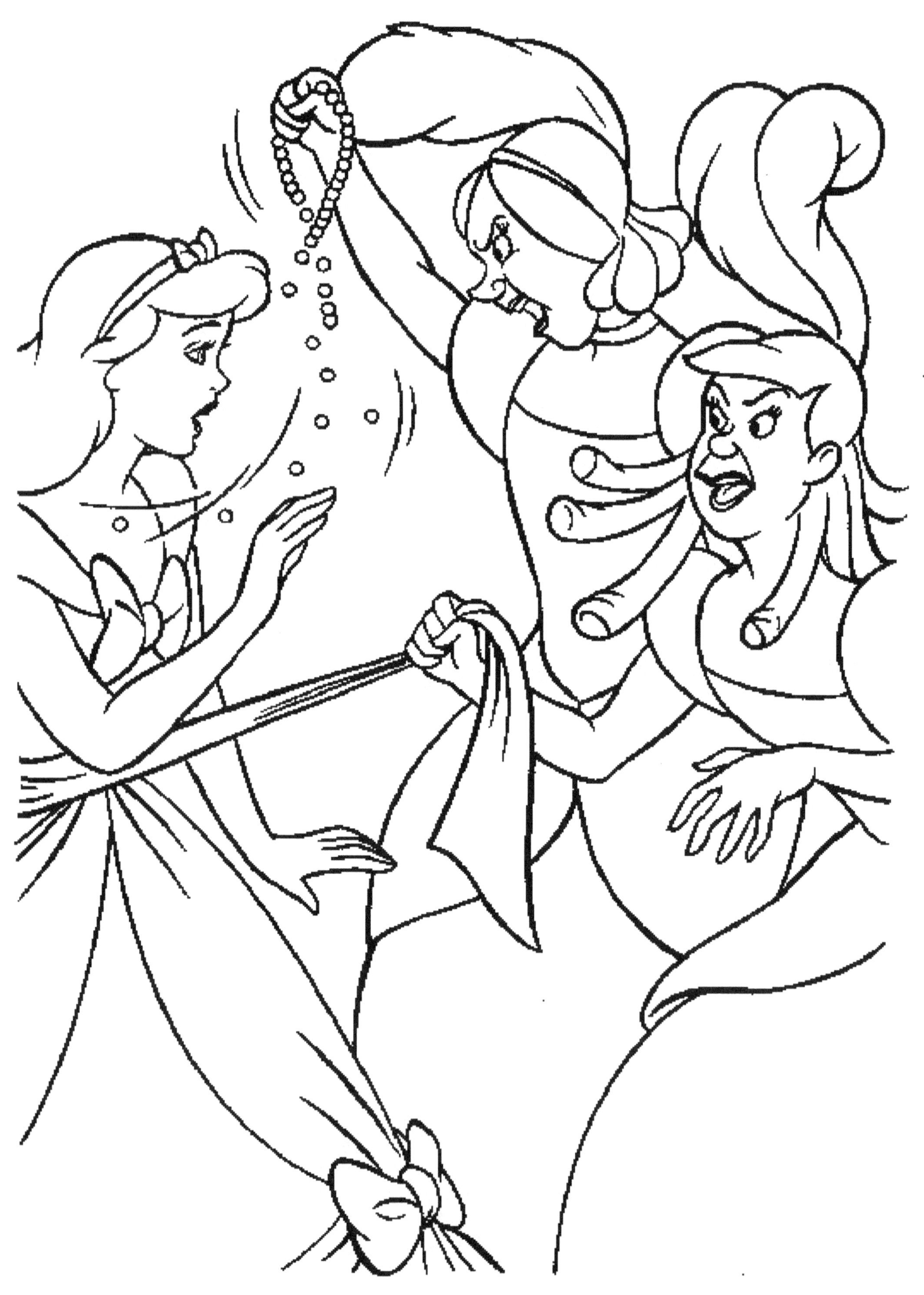

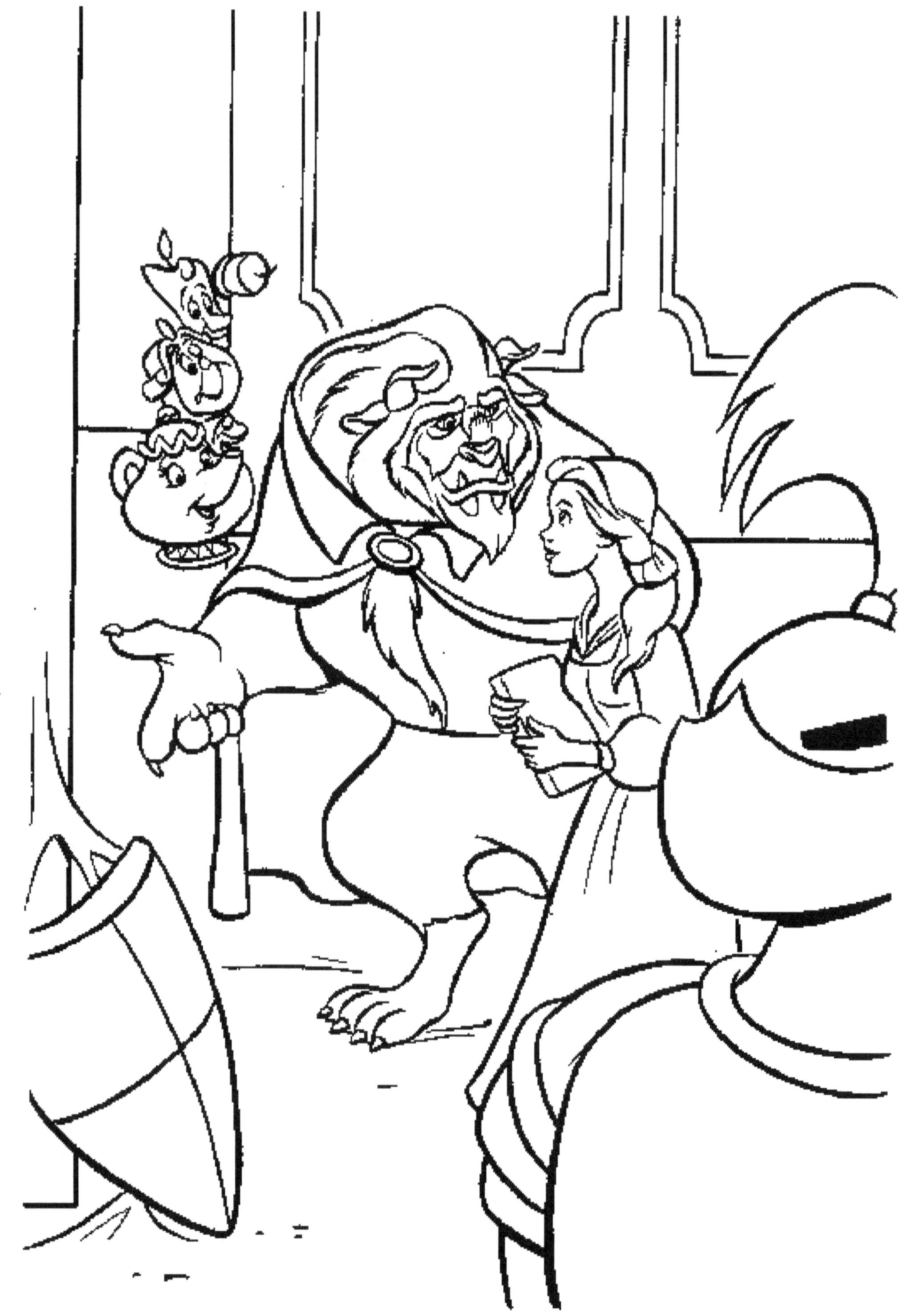

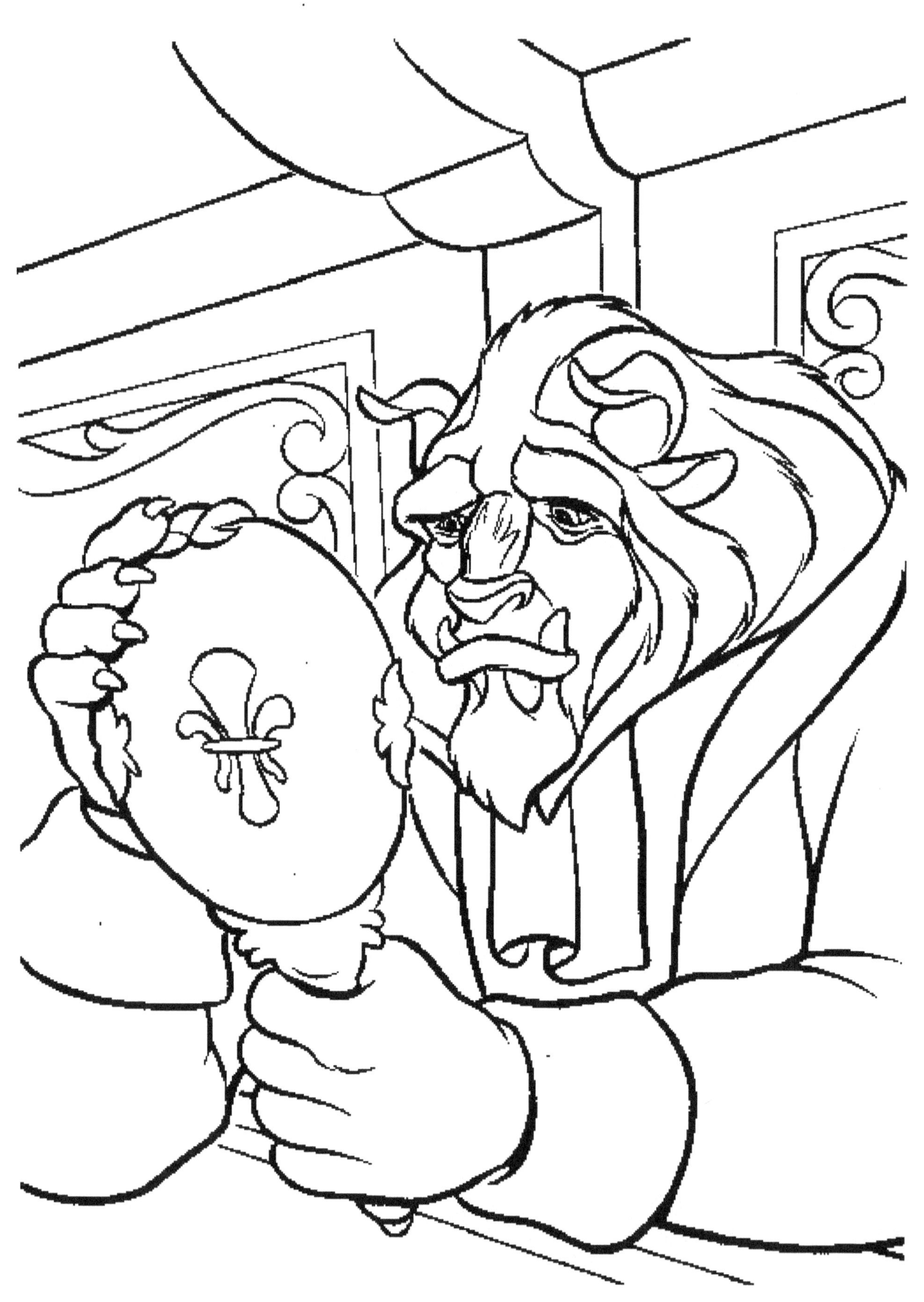

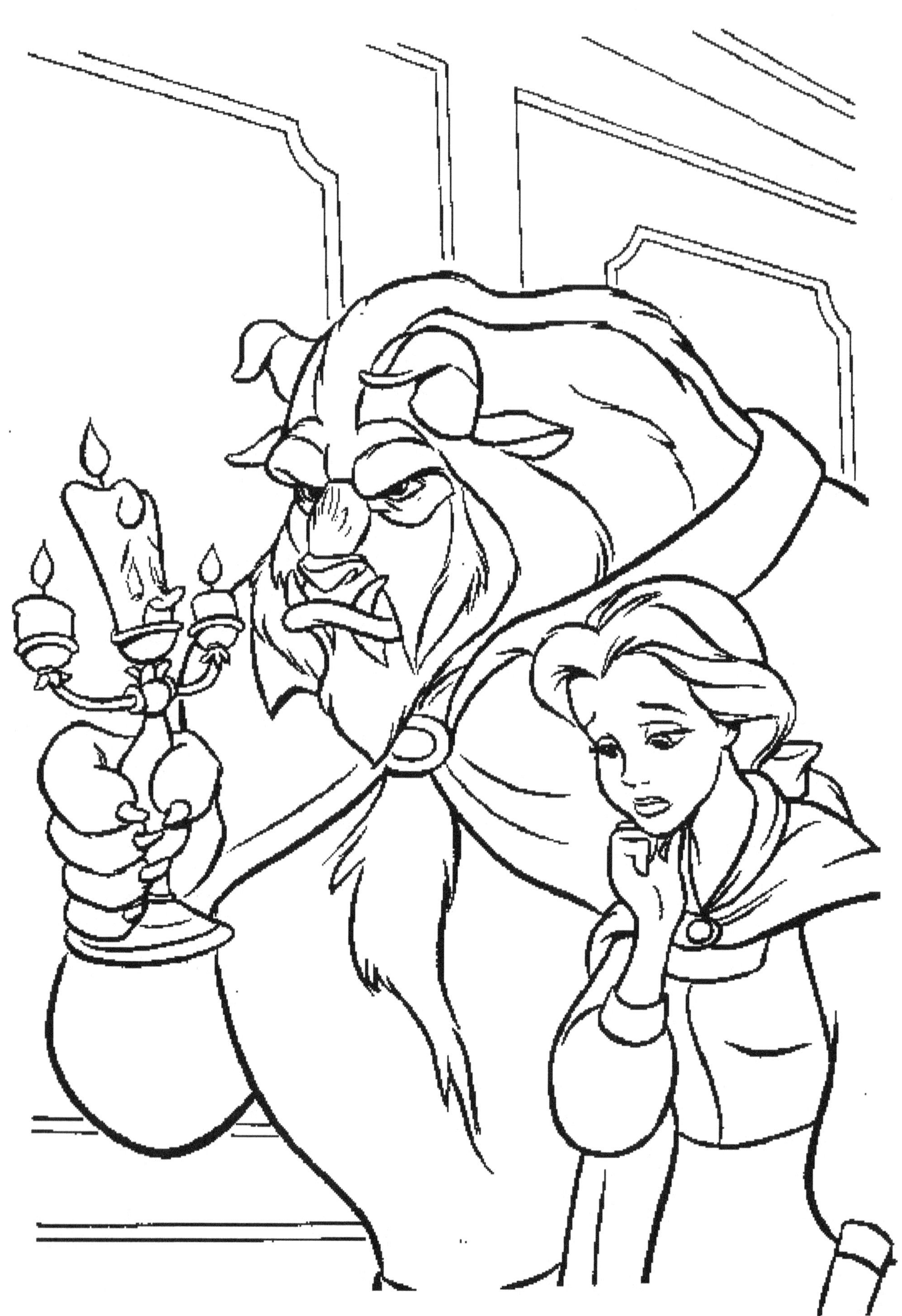

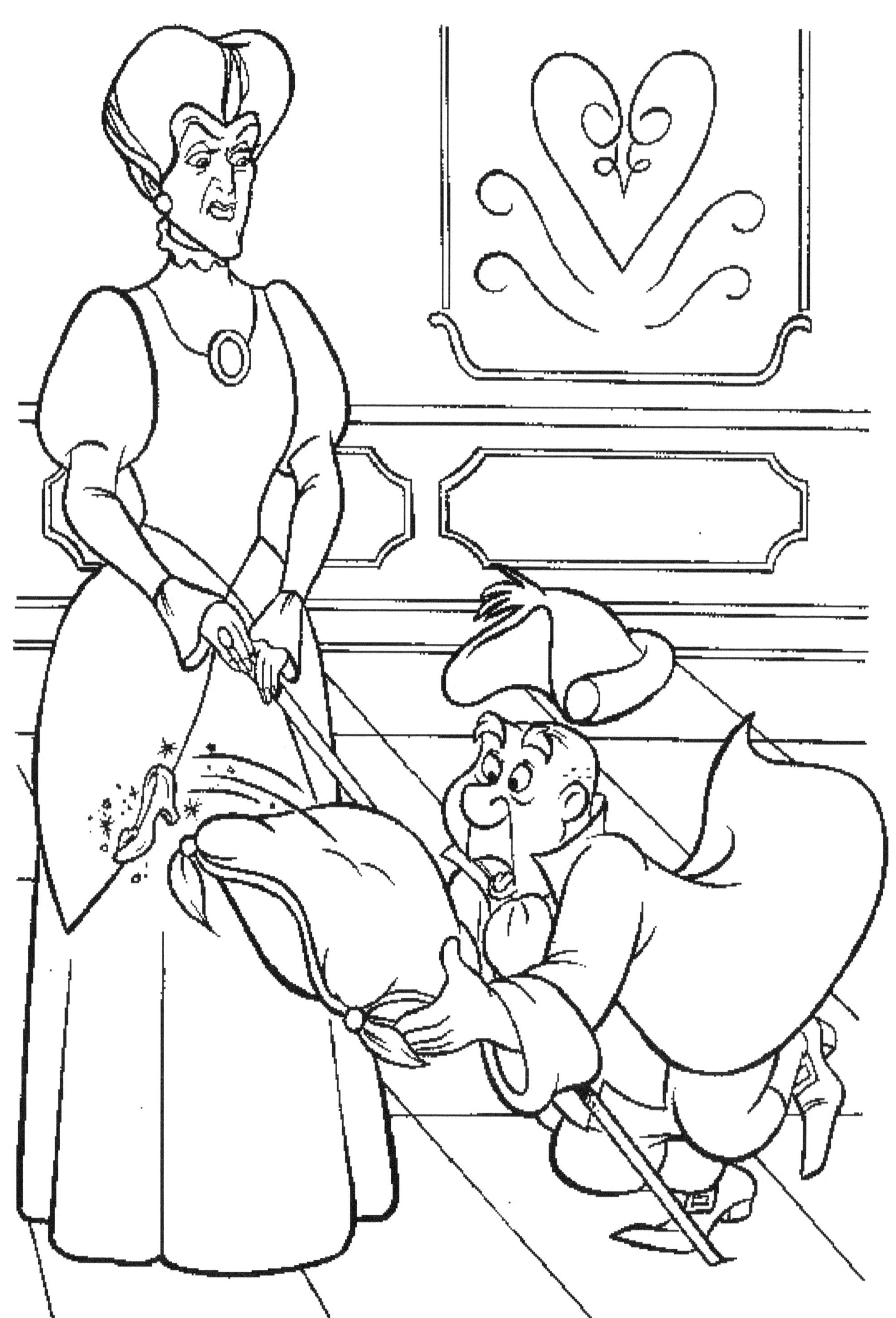

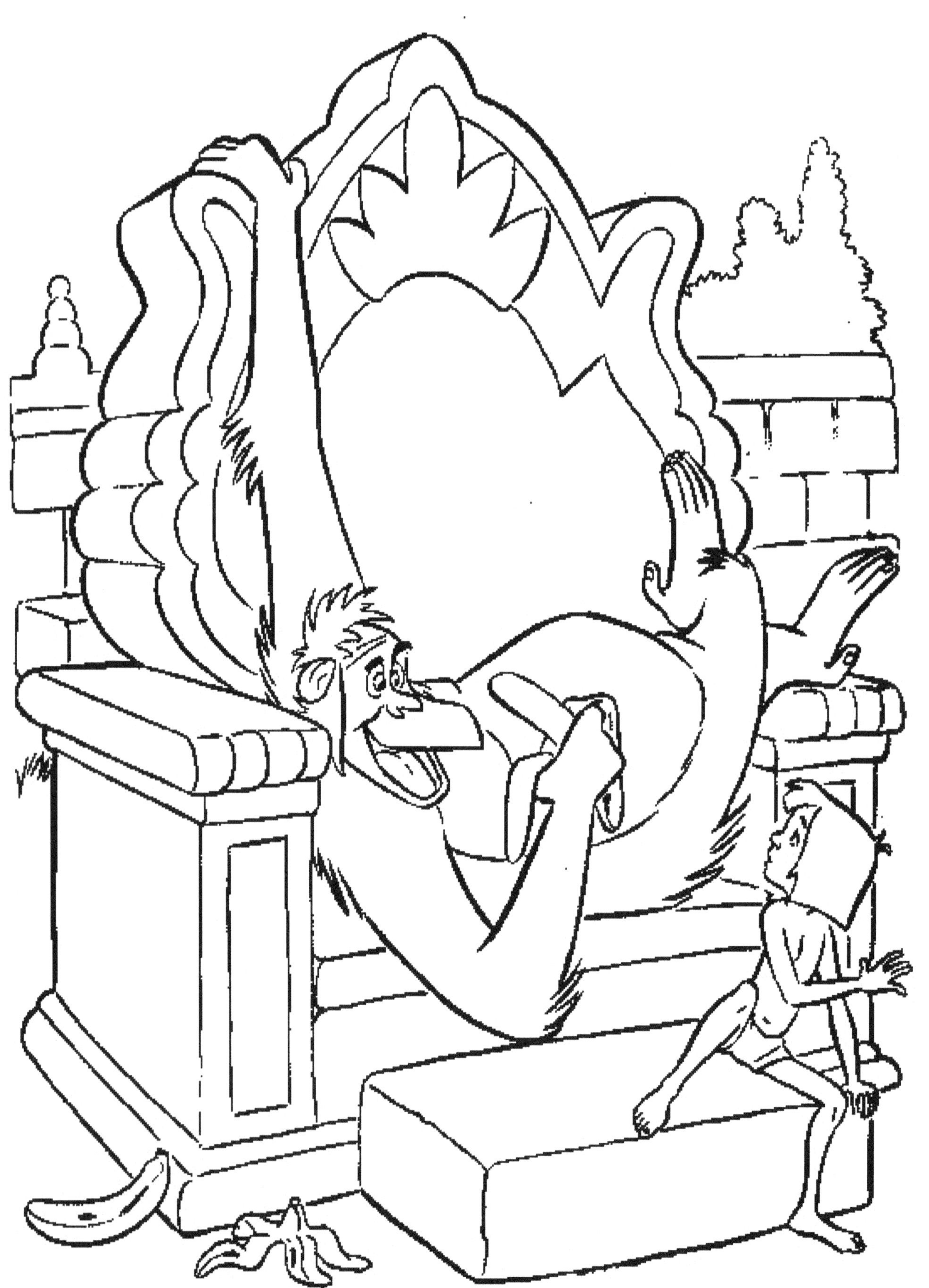

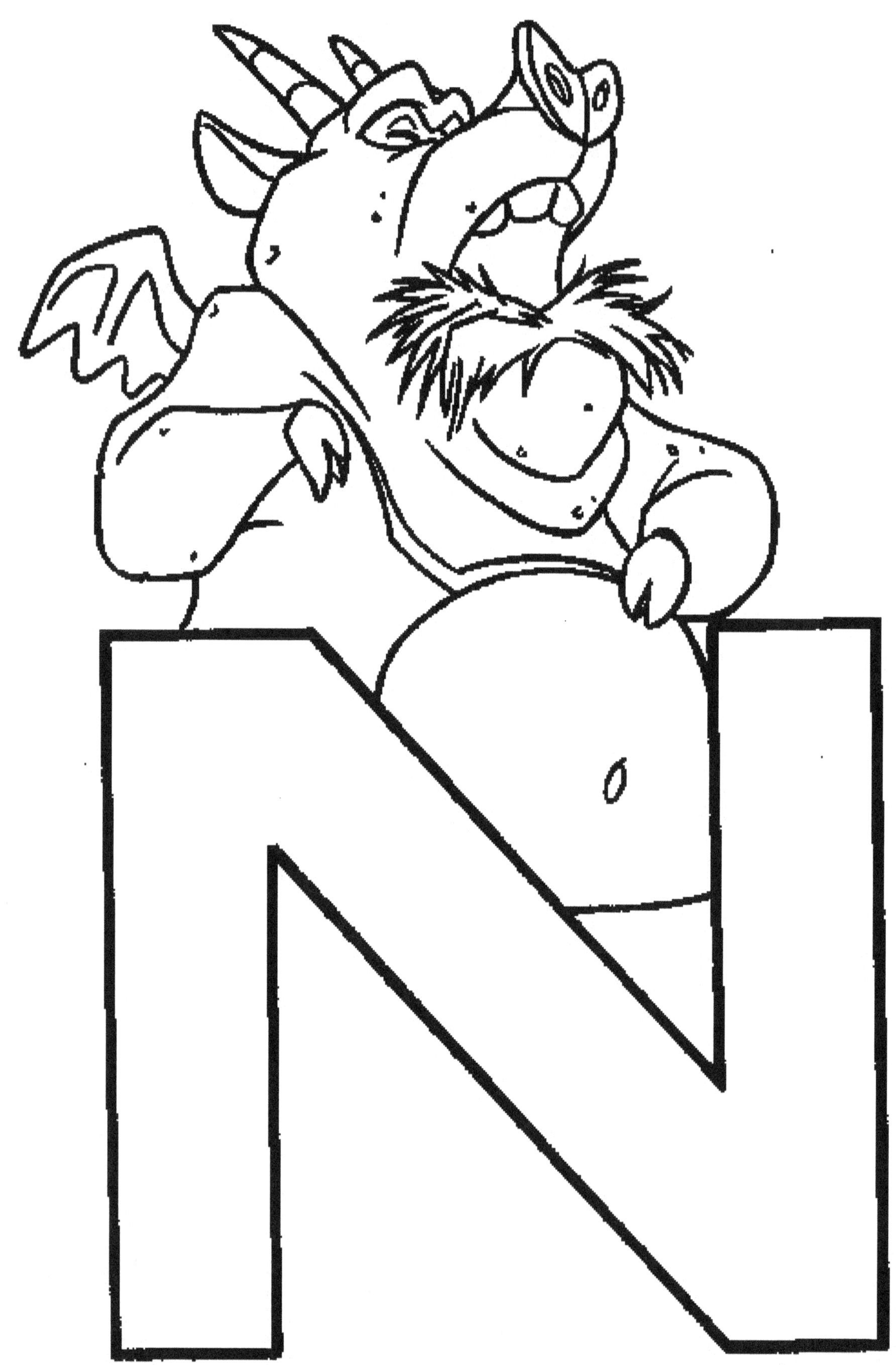

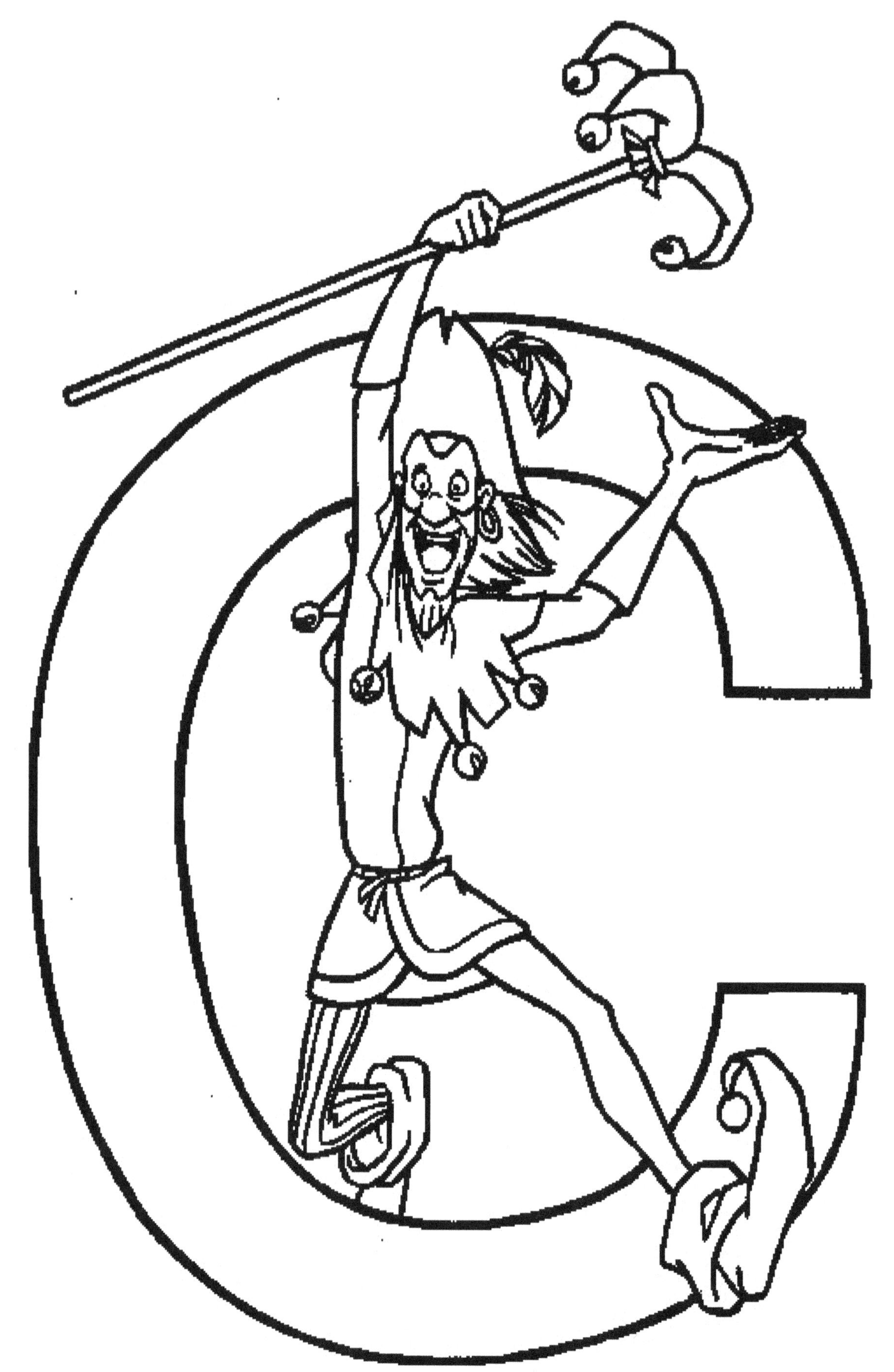

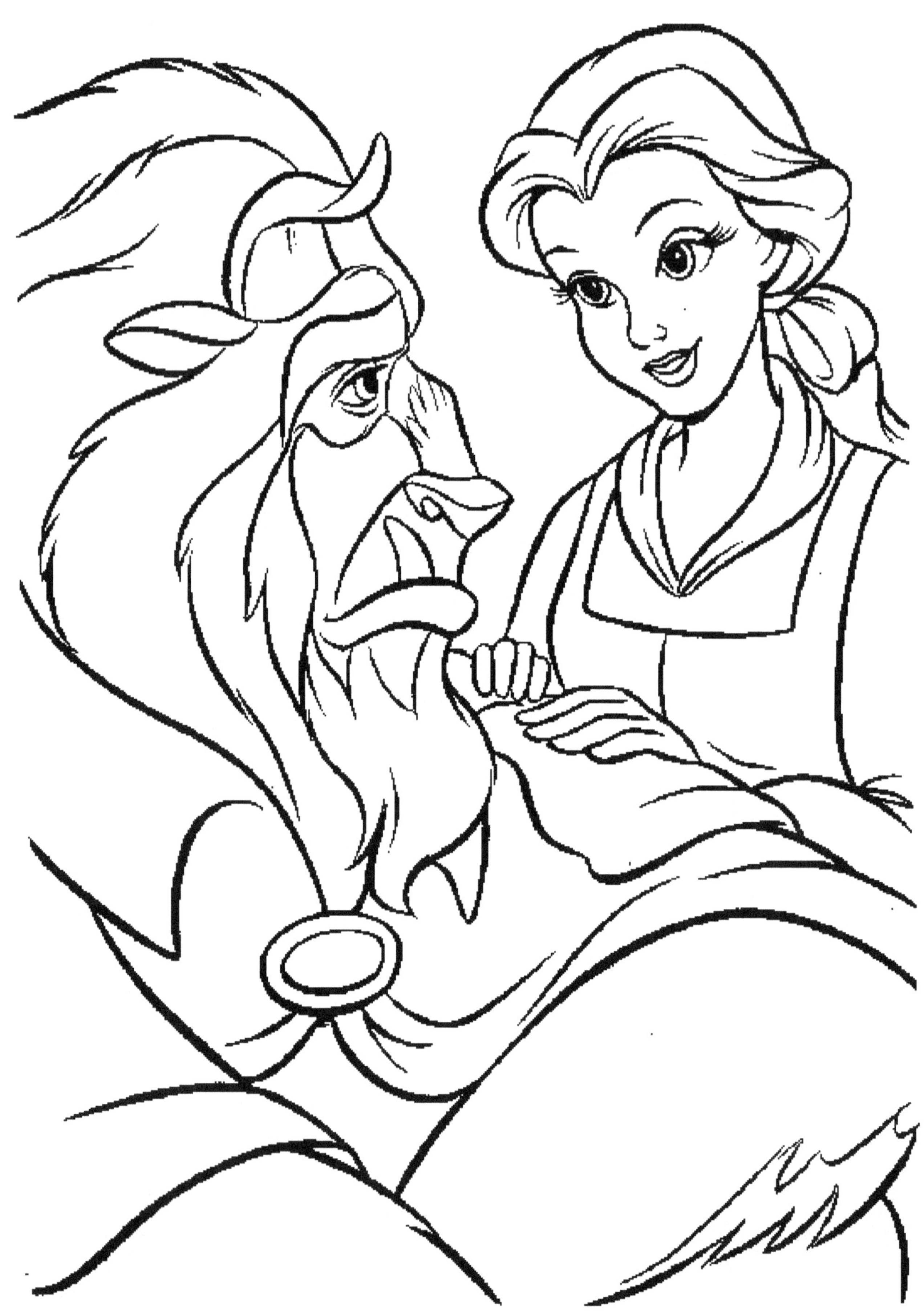

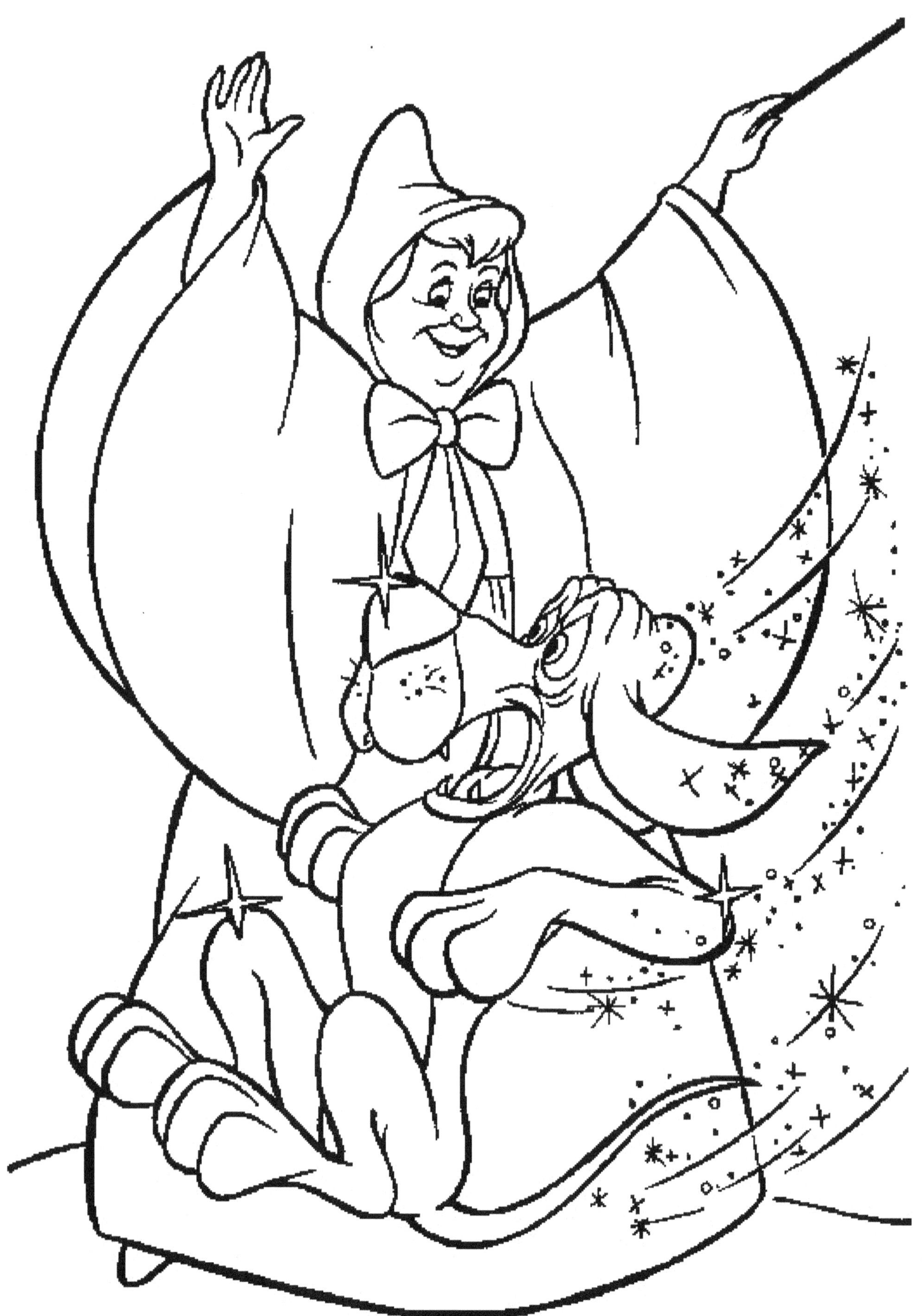

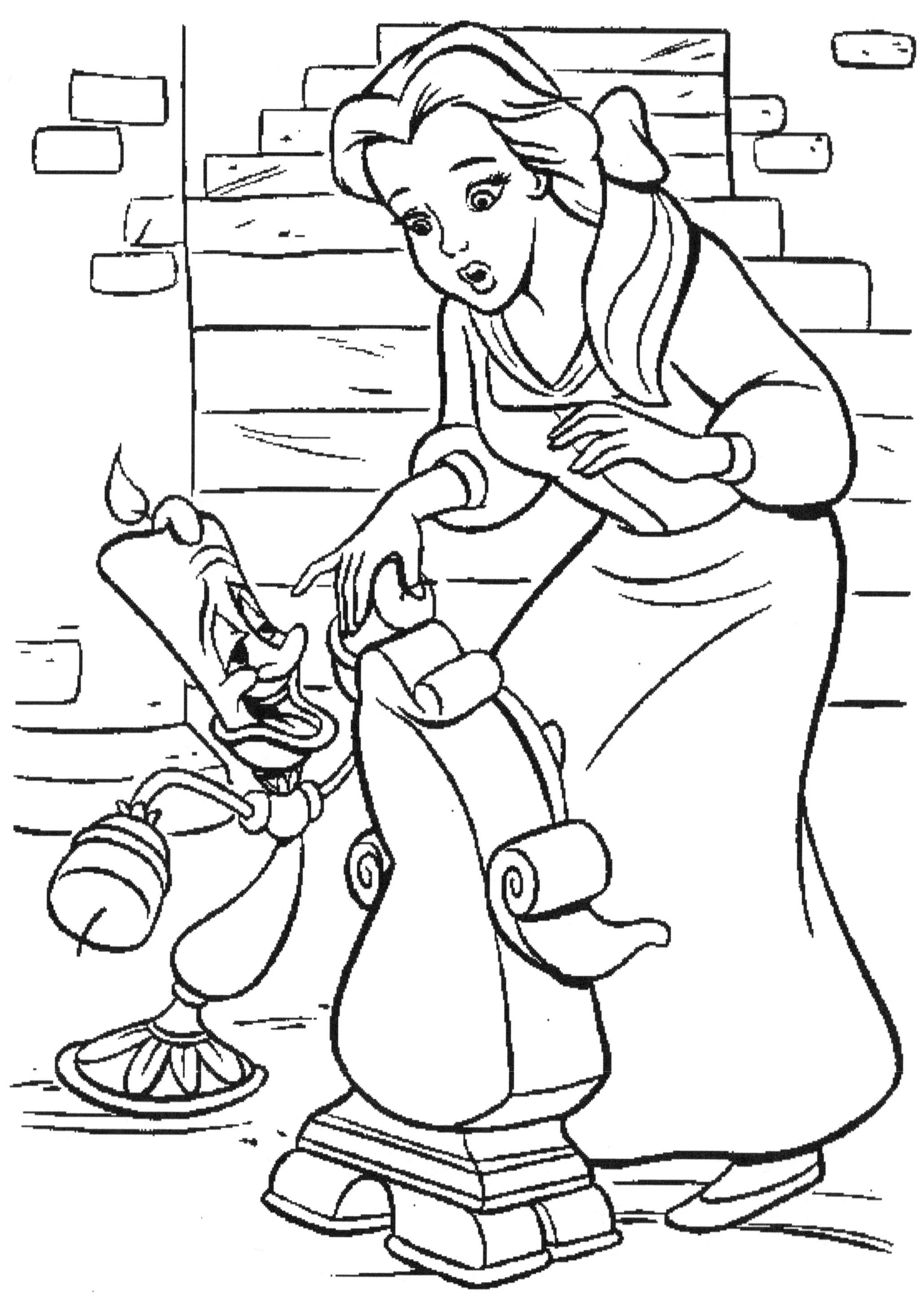

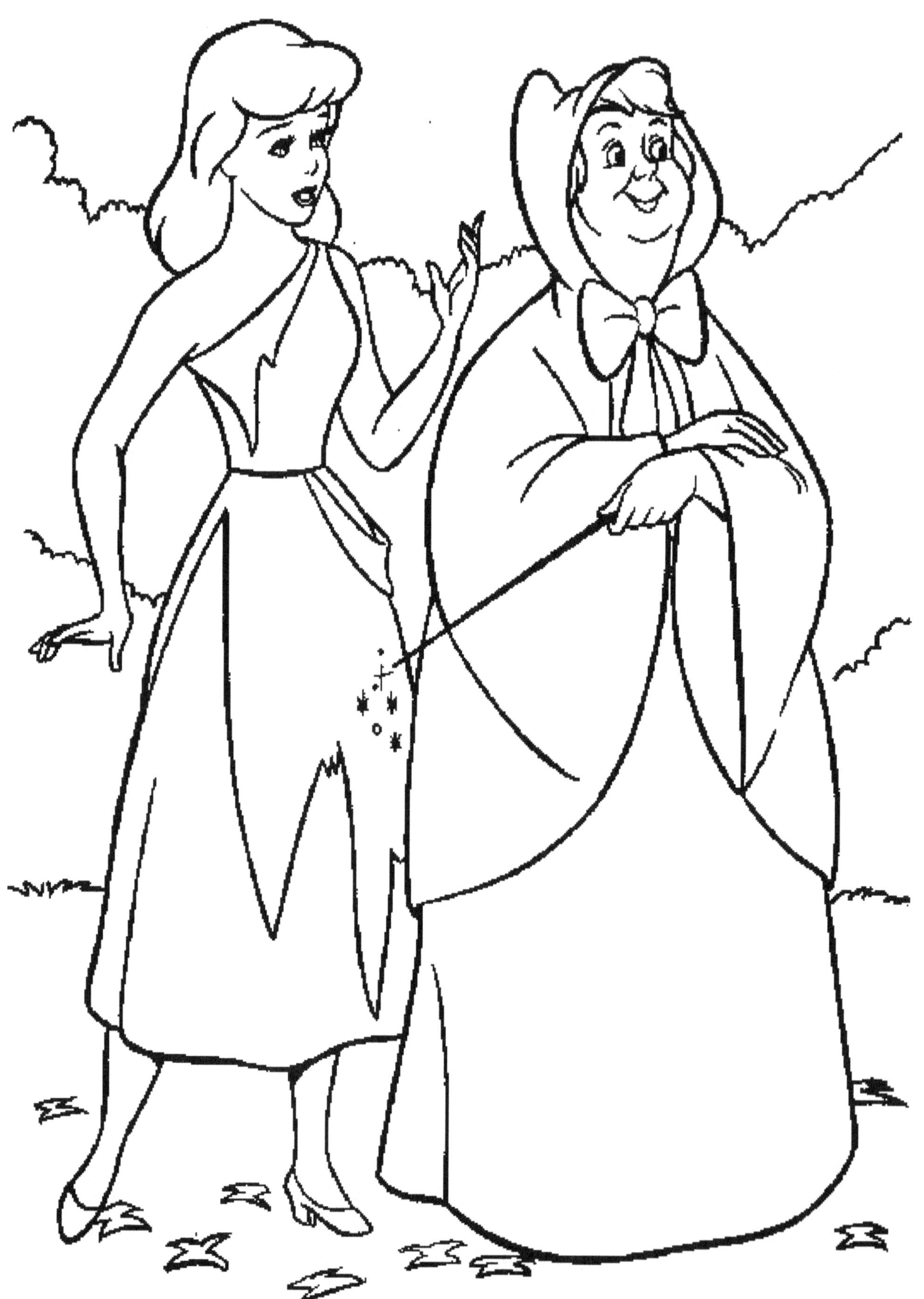

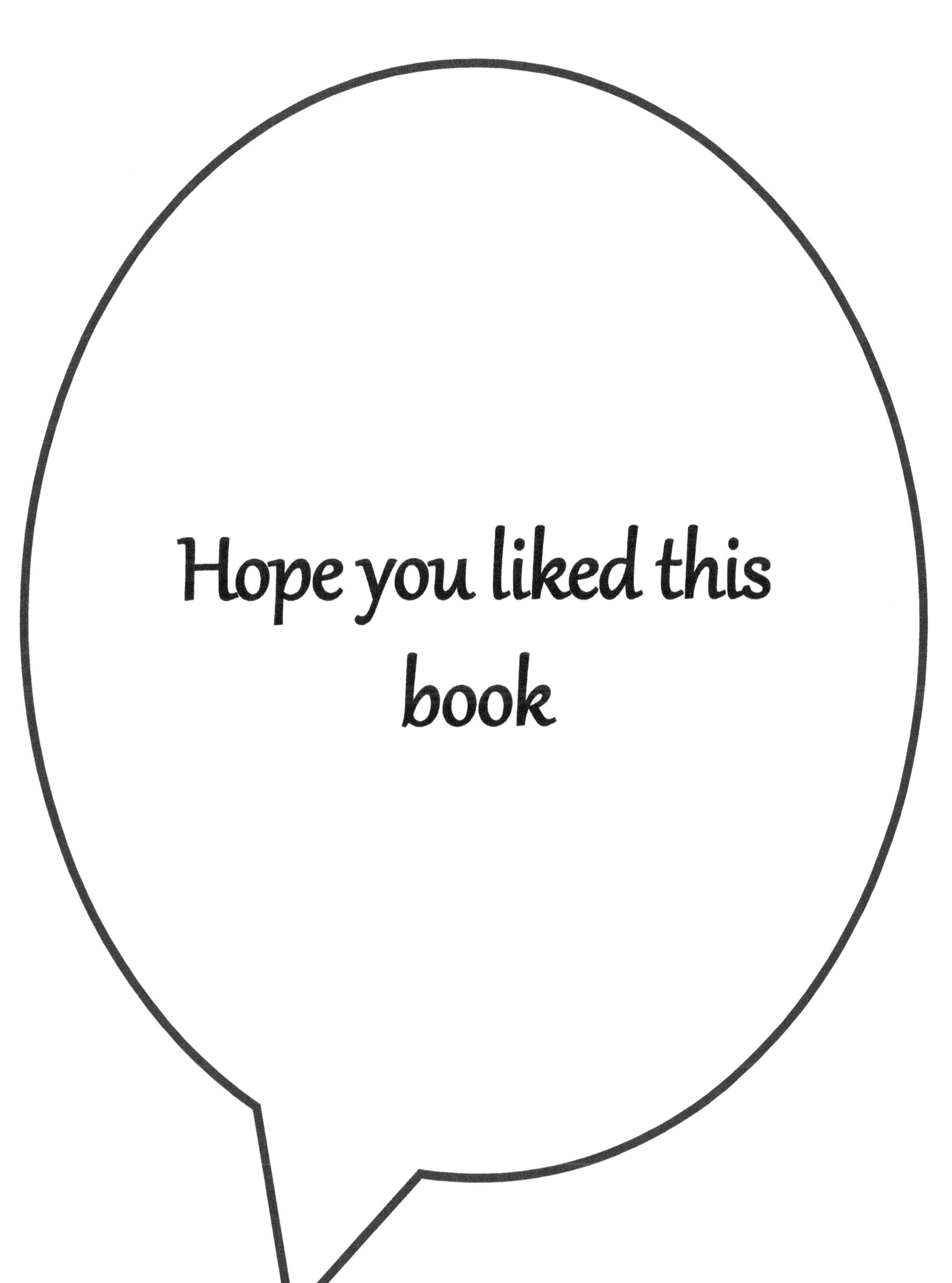

Hope you liked this
book

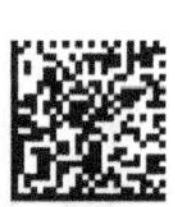